MW00917261

THE JOURNEY

Mastering the Art of Slowing Down Into a Beautiful Existence

CATHY TRINH

BALBOA.PRESS
A DIVISION OF HAY HOUSE

Balboa Press books may be ordered through booksellers or by contacting:

Balboa Press
A Division of Hay House
1663 Liberty Drive
Bloomington, IN 47403
www.balboapress.com
1 (877) 407-4847

ISBN: 978-1-9822-4684-6 (sc)
ISBN: 978-1-9822-4686-0 (hc)
ISBN: 978-1-9822-4685-3 (e)

Library of Congress Control Number: 2020908412

Printed in the United States of America.

Balboa Press rev. date: 06/22/2020

ADVANCE PRAISE FOR THE JOURNEY:

"MASTERING THE ART OF SLOWING DOWN INTO A BEAUTIFUL EXISTENCE

"Cathy is an extraordinary woman. We have been friends for many years. Along the way, we have shared some of life's greatest joys and deepest sorrows. Cathy has remained resilient and willing to face life head on regardless of the obstacles that have been placed in her way." **—Kristi Kettle** *Friend, Confidant, and "Forever Sponsor"*

"Cathy's metamorphosis is something to behold. I met Cathy on the arms of my longtime acquaintance that quite frankly, didn't deserve her. She exuded a warmth and depth that few people did--a certain type of tattooed and friendly "cool", which is a statement on her softness to the brutality of the world. Her softness which, to this day, is truly a strength. How could somebody who had been through so much injustice and cruelty be so light and airy? Cathy is an anomaly. So when she talks, listen. She's worth tuning in to." **—Bebe Gene**, *Entrepreneur | Productivity & Business Coach*

"Cathy Trinh is a free-spirited and talented soul that will keep you captivated throughout her book. She has opened her heart to the world to share her fears, doubts, power, and growth. Love my Big Sis to pieces." **—Caroline Trinh,** *Entrepreneur | Soul & Blood Sister*

"I'm so thrilled that Cathy has had the courage and commitment to not only persevere through so much adversity and hardship, but to write this book--sharing vulnerably and deeply the "*highs and lows*" of her life experiences and hard-earned wisdom in a way that inspires and empowers others. It's hard to believe that someone who has been through so much can embody as much joy and light as Cathy Trinh. As she shares her profound message, brilliant mind and loving spirit with audiences the world over, this book offers not only deeper insight into her inspiring journey, but simple and practical ways you can apply some of favorite gems to become who you've always known you could be." —**Scott Sargeant**, *Peak Performance Coach* & *TEDx Speaker "The Truth Will Set You Free" (Donovan Correctional)*

"Cathy Trinh is a beacon of light. Her book provides hope, encouragement and it truly impacts us all to be better. Cathy's message can help change your perspective on how to overcome adversity and ultimately become the best version of yourself. It's also a wonderful reminder of how resilient we are as individuals. It's a powerful story that will change your life." —**Suzan Nguyen,** *TEDx Speaker* "Be Better"| *Coach* | Author of *One Arm but Not Unarmed*

"Cathy is more than an inspiration. She has taken her incredible stories and turned them into lessons that will have a profound impact on your life. With the concept of H.O.L.Y. Moments, we transform out experiences with conscious slow living. Rarely do you find a book that changes the way you look at life, but even more so to find that changes the way you live your life. The Journey does both, and in a more powerful way than you ever thought possible." —**Kevin Hom**, *Entrepreneur* | *Real Estate Investor*

"This is a timely and essential book for our challenged world that we currently live in. Cathy is deeply inspiring and her book *The Journey: Mastering the Art of Slowing Down into a Beautiful Existence,* will not only bring healing, but will also expand your consciousness. She faces her fear as a way-shower to help you slow down into a more meaningful life." —**Brad Axelrad,** *Consultant & Event Producer Face Your Dragon*

"Cathy uses her own story of pain and recovery to show us the path to a better life. Her courage and resilience is a great lesson for everyone. This book will help you gain a deeper understanding of your own life and show you how to become your best self." —**Joe Nunziata,** *Speaker* | *Coach* | Author of *Heal the Deal, Chasing Your Life* and *Karma Buster*

"Cathy Trinh has faced tremendous obstacles, setbacks, and challenges in her life--many of which would have brought most people to their knees in defeat, yet she stands today triumphant. Her story is compelling, motivating, and challenging. I'm excited for her to share it with the world!" —**Randy Crane**, *Speaker* | Author of *Once Upon YOUR Time* and *Faith & the Magic Kingdom*

"Cathy's life is a heart-filled invitation for you to take another look at the world - to discover your prized gift and to live a life that is life-serving. If you're longing for deeper spirituality and inner-peace but feel that the craziness of life makes self-love challenging and at times impossible, this book is for you." —**Cary Hokama**, *Speaker* | *Executive Coach* | Author of *Own Your Self*

"Cathy is a powerhouse of a woman, and her story is a true light in this world. If you are looking to use your pain as a gift and transform your light, pick up this book and you will not only learn how, but be powerfully motivated to change. Thank you Cathy for writing this testimony of beauty for all the world to see." —**Franki Doll-Olinger**, *Speaker* | *Empowerment Coach* | Author of *The Five V's, Guide to Empowerment & Happiness, written with Love by a Modern Spiritual Warrior*

"Cathy's book is an inspirational read that takes a journey from infancy to adulthood with a Vietnamese child who allows you to share a path with her as she transforms into a successful woman. This book does show hope and promise for all of us who have been gifted to travel through this phenomenon called life." —**Anthony Brown**, RN, PHN, *Speaker* | Author of *From Park Bench to Park Avenue*

"Cathy's energy and presence today is a complete shift of who she once was and writes about in this book. Cathy shares about her life in ways human beings are uncomfortable and afraid in sharing theirs, opening up the hearts of her audience and being the light for others going through challenging times. Thank you for giving others the opportunity of a lifetime to get to know you."—**Calvin Hang,** *Owner | Co-founder, The Golden Marrow, Honey Belle*

"Cathy is an inspirational dynamo! When I first met her, she shared her life story and by the end of our talk I was so emotionally moved. Her perseverance is something that inspires me to be a better person in my own life." —**Allen Chen,** *Director of Photography-Firelight Media*

"Cathy Trinh's book stands out as an inspiration in overcoming harsh life lessons and obstacles. It stands true as a strong, meaningful example of how determination, hope, and love of one's self can mean so much more in the presence of hard life experiences." —**Shane Avila** *Film Producer* | Author of *Why The Butterfly Flew Away.*

"Cathy is a brave soul who shares her story and triumph over the most challenging and derailing events any person can experience. This includes her very personal stories of drug addiction at a young age due to careless post surgery medical care, sexual assault and kidnapping, toxic relationships and alcohol abuse to cope and battling and overcoming cancer. In her vulnerability she reveals how she healed and built a life of meaning. She now helps others to create amazing purposeful lives as both a talent recruiter and a growth mindset coach." —**Michael Devellano,** Author of *Automate & Grow*

"Cathy's contagious light and energy is shown through the stories her eyes tell and the pain she carries. I remember thinking that this was a woman who was going to become a force once she embraced the authentic beauty and power within herself. Through the years I have watched her become expansive within her story, leaning into the struggles and embracing her triumphs. With each leveling up internally, Cathy has brought her story of survival and ability to thrive to share with the world around her - inspiring others with the opportunities hidden within the darkness of life's trials. Cathy's story and philosophy of "Slowing Down" with her trio of Slow-Care, Self-Care, and Soul-Care will empower so many to take a breath and find their way back to themselves." —**Dr. Kate Truitt,** Award-winning *Licensed Clinical Psychologist | Havening Techniques Certified Trainer*

"Cathy is a Survivor. She has been through so much. She has come out so much better and stronger. She is an inspiration to everyone. Anyone going through hard times, this book will remind you to slow down and not let the world overwhelm you." —**John Potter** *USMC – retired marine*

"Cathy has helped me begin my meditation journey. Having her professional input and feedback has helped me begin on the right track to learn how to live a slower life by living in the sunlight of the spirit and my heart." —**Jennie Tran**

"I was keen on slowing down my mindset to change my life, to learn new skills, and Cathy fought for me to achieve that aim." —**Caroline Navarro**

"I was fortunate to have Cathy on my team. Cathy is not just a transformed human being; she is a life coach, a mentor, she is inspirational!" —**Don Willets**

"Cathy was my absolute favorite mindset coach I have ever worked with!" —**Tan Nguyen**

"Positive energy is *EVERYTHING.* And Cathy has that energy. For change." —**Rod Espudo**

"Although I haven't met Cathy personally, her online presence, messages and pictures have made my life better." —**David Lau**

"Cathy is professional, passionate and extremely diligent in her work. Vince Lombardi, coach for the Green Bay Packers, once said: "*The price of success is hard work, dedication to the job at hand, and the determination that whether we win or lose, we have applied the best of ourselves to the task at hand."* I was fortunate to have Cathy on my team. Cathy is not just a recruiter; she is a life coach, a mentor, and inspirational! —**Jeorjii Cruz**

"Cathy is an exquisite beautiful soul & spirit that exponentially resonates and attracts far and near. She has this ability to reach and lift up all through her simplicity & authenticity by leaps and bounds!!" —**Keith Lott**

"Cathy has had such a positive influence in my life. I look forward to hearing what she has to say daily for inspiration"—**Laurence Fulton**

"Cathy cares. I feel her powerful, positive and transforming attitude and presence daily." —**Daniel Wansten**

"I've known Cathy for over 15 years. Cathy experienced a lot of bumps, detours and challenges along the way that would have debilitated others, but she emerged from those years with a strength and passion that have been sharpened like an iron in a forge. Her experience has given her undeniable credibility and wisdom that cries out to be shared." —**Dan Sakimoto**

"Sometimes, all you need is someone to justify that your existence in this world has a purpose and that's exactly what Cathy made me feel. After meeting her, I started to feel invincible, that I could conquer the world." —**Jonah Rodriguez**

"Cathy's inner light shines. Every day. She allows her light to bring out light in those she meets and cares about. Beautiful soul." —**Kathleen Sheppard**

"I can probably write a chapter, but I'll keep it short. My personal friendship with Cathy has changed me in such a positive way. I shared some things going on in my life and she gave me ideas and solutions tailored to my needs. I applied those suggestions and I not only feel amazing but I have such a positive outlook on my life and future. Cathy is amazing and I truly value our friendship." —**Steve Ruddy**

Love what you're reading?

Tell me what has been a powerful catalyst in your life or influenced you to change in positive and transformative ways? I would love to hear how your intentions, actions, and life are changing by what you are experiencing and reading. I invite you to connect with me at:

Cathy@CathyTrinh.com

CONTENTS

SPECIAL ACKNOWLEDGMENTS

To my parents, *Mai Huynh* and *Khanh Trinh*, whose personal journey as immigrants helped me see the pain as well as suffering attached to this phenomenon of life. Their story will now help others avoid this pain and create more peaceful lives.

To my son, *Noah*, who instinctively lives in a state of flow, ease and trust. He has shown me what love truly is. He has taught me about my own inner strength, resilience and inspired me to build a life for us both that I did not think was possible. To my sweet, intelligent, and amazing bonus daughter, *Margaret*, thank you for paving the path to a bright future for both yourself and Noah who looks up to you immensely. I love you both with all my heart!

To my *friends & family*, who have shown me unconditional love and support along the way. Thank you for allowing me to feel the power of possibilities with true love and community.

To my *dear friend, Ly Hoang-Schmidt,* who I trusted to witness my healing, growth and developmental process of this book before sharing with the eyes of the world – I am deeply grateful to her for the long editorial labors, her spiritual depth and the passion she poured into the raw manuscripts of this book. To my wonderful *friends, Kathleen Sheppard and Kevin Hom,* for your suggestions and encouragement. To *Thanh Nguyen,* for your friendship and added special inspiration to help me uncover and shed light on the most critical battle with sex & love addiction during the age of the internet and modern day society.

To my *sisters, Caroline & Anna*, for your unbreakable bond of devotion and sisterhood. *Caroline,* thank you for the being the rock and holding my hand through my journey with cancer. *Anna*, thank you for the strength you've shown me by simply being the responsible and independent woman that you are. To *Charlize,* the sweetest loving niece an Auntie can ask for. Your smiles, love and light brightens up every room you enter. I love you to the moon and back! To *Rev. Jim Schibsted,* for your love and believing in me. To *Kristi Kettle,* for being my "*Forever Sponsor,*" friend and confidant. To *Bebe Gene,* for friendship and strength to help pick me up and drag me through the mud to a higher self.

To *Miss Cathy,* for taking my daily outreach calls with kindness and compassion, and loving us all daily. Thanks to you, both Noah and I know how to be decent pet owners and give difficult pets a chance for once. To *Kelly G.,* for choosing me to be our fearless leader at the Friday morning meetings. Your female wisdom and have smiles make me coming back, *regardless.* To *Helen,* for miraculously coming into my life and confirming my life's purpose on the chosen path of recovery. I searched for you all my life. Simply, thank you for your strength and courage to battle the disease of addiction.

We're in this together.

To *Markus, Noah's dad,* thank you for inspiring me to write a book and believing in me since day one. Without your life's struggle living with Bipolar Manic Depression, the 51/50's you've encountered, your wisdom from the prison yard and gift of Noah's life – I wouldn't be the woman I am today. I also probably wouldn't have made it out alive with my own struggle with addiction. Thank you for intervening in 2002 with your love and sharing the message with a fellow addict/alcoholic. *I appreciate you and the life lessons I've gained.* Lastly, but most importantly to *Carol, Markus' mom* you are one tough lady. Without you I wouldn't have made it through some of those dark times while going through those manic rollercoasters. Thank you for your suggestion of reading "An Unquiet Mind," I own the book, but haven't completed it yet, since I was so busy living our own bipolar madness. I love you.

Love you all.

With Love and Gratitude,

CATHY TRINH

"The most important thing is to try and inspire people so that they can be great in whatever they want to do." **—Kobe Bryant**

FOREWORD BY CATHY TRINH'S SON

NOAH FALIANO, Age 11

My name is Noah Faliano. I am 11 years old and in the fifth grade. I love to play soccer. I also enjoy playing video games online with my friends after school. I get good grades and I love all my teachers! I am very good at building Legos and want to be an *aerospace engineer* when I grow up. All my friends know that I'm a happy kid, but not all of them know about my Mom and Dad. You see, both my parents have gotten really sick while I have been growing up. My Mom had cancer and my Dad has a mental illness. There have been times when my Dad is gone for a while…I feel really sad, sometimes abandoned. My Mom loves me so much though. Even when she was sick, her love made my fear and sadness go away. Lately, things have been better. I can play soccer with my Dad again. My Mom and I don't go to the hospital as much. I feel a lot happier. It just took both of them a long time to feel better too.

In this book you'll learn a little about my Mom, Cathy. Actually, you're going to learn a lot about my Mom because she is not afraid to share her story! I'm so proud that she talks about what she has gone through because people, even strangers, tell me how my Mom inspires them. She is my *Superhero*. She is my *Super Mom*. My Mom is very creative. She comes up with wacky ideas all the time. Her ideas are like pop-up ads on the internet or my YouTube videos. It's been a little embarrassing, because my Mom is good at capturing funny Moments of me to post them on the internet. Good thing she has me…because with me by her side, she says that *I am her firewall.*

I love my Mom. She has gone through a lot in her life. I have seen her at her best. She is the happiest when her recruiting business is doing well. It's those good times when we can afford to buy a Christmas tree. I remember one time she got really creative one year. She used a broomstick covered with a blanket and strung some Christmas lights around it. I've also seen her at her lowest, like when she was in the hospital, she couldn't talk because of tubes draining blood from her throat after her cancer surgery. She wasn't at her happiest *then*, but she still knew how to put a smile on my face. I always smile when she smiles.

On the other hand, my Dad has a mental illness. The doctors call it Bipolar Manic Depression. Since I was a little kid, two years old I think, he has been gone from my life for chunks at a time. I have visited him in mental hospitals, sometimes jails too, but I'm not allowed to see him when he is in prison. That has happened a few times too. Today, he is doing much better. I still love my Dad, even after everything that has happened. I'm told that he can't control what happens when he gets sick, or sometimes when he gets sick. I've tried to remember that.

One thing that my Dad did give me to last forever was an older half-sister. I call her sister Margaret. She lives in Oregon. I don't see her all the time, but she knows what it's like to have parents that have hard days too. Her Mom struggles in different ways than my Mom, as she has told me, but she says that I am loved more than I know. She made it to college. I want to be able to pay for college like she did, with good grades and scholarships. She inspires me. I love my sister Margaret very much. I wish that when she would visit me, she could stay forever. She wishes for that too.

Above all, my Mom is a *superhero* that doesn't need a cape. She has inspired me a lot in my life. I know that she can inspire you too. Even though we had some hard days, I know I am a good kid. My sister says that I'm the sweetest, most caring boy that she knows. I know that means a lot. Without my Mom, I would not be where I am: safe, happy and loved. I'm excited to have my Mom with me as I grow up. She says that I can do anything in life I put my mind to. If both my parents can get through their struggles, I can too. I hope this book inspires you like my Mom inspires me.

Love,
Noah

SS

"Health is the greatest gift, contentment the greatest wealth, faithfulness the best relationship."

—Buddha

FOREWORD & DEDICATION BY CATHY TRINH

Thank you in advance for picking up this book and giving me the opportunity to share my life's journey with you. With over 15 years in the making, writing this book has allowed me to heal, move forward, and hopefully make an impact in your life too. For that, I am forever grateful.

This book was written from the immense struggles that I endured on this winding journey of life I have walked. From the lessons of healing, growth, self-reflection, self-excavation, from rebuilding my dignity, and self-worth from within, I aspired to catalogue this journey in a way to impact others. This book was written from the depth of my heart's calling, in the spirit of hope that embodies my Soul. Through this book, I dedicate my words for others experiencing any kind of struggle.

My journey will touch your heart. To all of you facing job transitions; going through break ups, battling with addictions, concerned with your health, dealing with emotional and spiritual abuse, seeking safe harbor to open up, going through major life changes, rebuilding your own life, creating your own path as business owners, raising children, reconciling your own childhood, growing or sinking in relationships, seeking self-sovereignty, self-autonomy and spiritual guidance – I hear you, I feel you, I've BEEN you.

For everyone who feels with their heart, gives with their soul, believes with their vision, who are ready to receive the same endless abundant love you give, this book is for you. For those who are ready to tap into that divine inner peace that is Source, joy, love and beauty within you – I'm so glad you're here. Welcome.

My greatest fulfilling life purpose is to help others unblock self-limiting beliefs to gain confidence in creating the life they deserve. I help men and women tap into their own intuitive gifts to trust their decisions in building the life they love.

I hope to be an inspirational '*beacon of hope*' for those in similar situations as my past, because even though I am a working professional,

I have experienced great struggles, downfalls, suffering, life lessons, as well as similar abuse as many did. I hope that by sharing my life story so intimately as a testimonial, others will see an example of how I picked myself up from my rock bottom. I want you to discover how to rebuild and how you can provide for your family as I did. I developed stronger coping skills, recovered from those traumatic situations, worked on the deeper internal spiritual work to truly heal from within to turn into the person I am proud to be today. I hope that this book will be a testament that, if I can overcome my hardships, then you can too.

From my heart to yours, I am deeply honored to share this manuscript as a blueprint or roadmap for you to use as a flashlight to help you see more clearly, stumble a little less, and enjoy the view on your journey.

With all my love,
Cathy

This book was written for those who have lived a hectic life, worked hard, struggled, suffered loss, been let down, forgotten, pushed aside and ignored. For those who have fought, battled, persevered or recovered - I stand alongside you to encourage you, inspire you, strengthen you and challenge you. We can rise above together with knowledge, wisdom and truth – most importantly you will live the extraordinary life you love by *slowing down into a beautiful existence.*

—Cathy Trinh

"The journey of a thousand miles begins with one step." —**Lao Tzu**

MY WINDING JOURNEY: CHILDHOOD TO ADULTHOOD

This book is based on real-life events. Firsthand stories from my refugee parents & my own personal testimony.

I was born in 1977 in Binh Minh, Saigon after the Vietnam War. By 1979, my family made the decision to flee the country due to the communist regime and downturn of the economy. After four failed attempts, my teenage parents and I were smuggled out of the country by a small fishing vessel. We set sail on a seven day voyage on the Pacific Ocean based on faith alone. By God's grace, we were rescued and sought refuge in the Kuku Islands' refugee camp in Indonesia. We spent nine months in the camp, feverishly waiting for a permanent home somewhere on the horizon.

By April 1979, our family made a connection with my grandmother, who had already settled in Orange County, California. Our sponsorship process to the United States began. We made our way to the U.S. in 1980 and luckily to "*The O.C.*" (Orange County, California) where we still reside today. In 1982 and then in 1985, I became an older sister two times over, with my sisters, Caroline and Anna, both born in Orange County. I am the eldest and the only child in my family who traveled across seas by boat to arrive here with scars from war time. Although I don't cognitively remember our treacherous experiences, I know the memories are imprinted in my subconscious mind and have affected my survival responses as an adult.

Our family lived in a gang-infested area in Southern California. While growing up in a blue-collared immigrant home was not easy, we turned out to be pretty good kids. I was a good student, a nerdy clarinet musician and an average basketball player. Mom was a seamstress. My Dad drove the metro city bus. After 35 years of hard work, Dad was recognized and acknowledged by winning an award for being the *"Best of the Best"* metro bus operator out of 7,500 operators in the entire Los Angeles Metro line. My parents worked hard and sacrificed a lot to provide for us. They also struggled to raise three rebellious girls.

My weight fluctuated at age thirteen, when on the Junior High Varsity Basketball team, I suffered a major injury to my right knee cap, which led to my first hospitalization. I gained weight, had body image issues and developed an eating disorder. I began my journey into an addiction using dangerous weight loss drugs prescribed by my physician with effects I'm sure that still last to this day. From that point on, I spent six years in a mental prison with the painstaking need to numb each feeling, anxiety, and problem I faced. My mind, as well as my body recklessly moved fast due to the relentless effects of the drugs. I couldn't slow down. For a long time, I rapidly followed my impulses. I couldn't slow down to take control of my life.

I became a lost girl.

In 1992 (age 15), I was a victim of a rape by an older man while waiting at a bus stop. For the next 20 years, I trudged through life riddled with fear, shame and guilt. I kept that secret until I was ready to tell my story when I turned 39 years old. My life changed dramatically from that event and I fell easily into a victimhood mentality. I was one of the 2% statistic that did not know my attacker. I refer to this sexually violent incident as

"The Awakening" because it aggressively forced me to awaken on so many levels after the suffering and pain into healing.

I stayed lost, but more so didn't want to be found.

From 1993 to 2002, I struggled with addiction to alcohol and party drugs, as well as developed addictions to food, relationships, codependency, and sex – trying desperately to find unconditional love. When I started opening up about my life, the sexual assault, having one epiphany after another, I knew I was on to something. I knew why I had chosen the path my feet were on.

By the end of 2002, I hit my first rock bottom. I was spiritually bankrupt emotionally, physically, mentally and spiritually. I entered into recovery to figure out how to quiet down the voices in my head and what was going on inside my mind. What I didn't realize was that it was the beginning of a much deeper Soul journey.

It led me down to a much higher path of self-healing, self-discovery and self-love.

One day at a time, I slowly recovered from a hopeless state of mind from drug and alcohol addiction. I finally had a breakthrough after deep self-reflection by working the program, a lot of soul searching and healing from trauma. I didn't start to heal until I finally opened up about the road I trudged and the traumas I encountered on my journey. I also discovered other pathways to spiritual enlightenment, sobriety and healing other than the 12 steps in recovery. I learned how to slow down, release self-limiting beliefs, shift my mindset and release old trauma wounds with new healing techniques called Havening Touch and other methods. I also attended the Landmark Forum breakthrough courses to learn how to let go of the past, walked on fire with Tony Robbin's *Unleash the Power*, mastered breath work, and experienced empowerment through other transformational leadership programs. Ultimately through years of my own self-healing journey, it became clear that the man who raped me years prior had suffered from a mental and spiritual alcoholic malady. From that point on, I prayed that it would never happen to anyone else. From acceptance, there was forgiveness. I was finally able to forgive him and move forward. It was quite an eye-opener for me.

I worked hard and I dug deep. *The truth is:* The Landmark Forum helped transform me and shift my perspective in life. I used other programs and tools to help experience breakthroughs, slow me down and learn how to live an extraordinary life. On my Landmark registration form, I wrote *"I want to have a breakthrough in communication and learn how to slow my life down from everything I was running away from."* And I did just that.

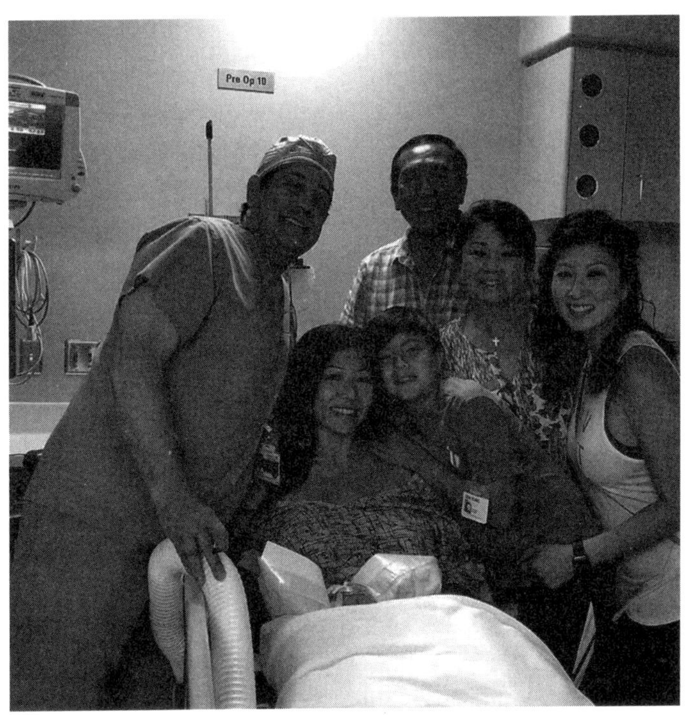

In March 2018, at age 40, I received a diagnosis that changed my life forever. Cancer made its way into my body. This was the beginning of a whole new level of self-awareness that forced me to elevate my thinking and slow down. I fought hard, regained control and experienced multiple miraculous spiritual awakenings on my recovery journey. I am happy to report I won the battle with my health concerns and accumulated a wealth of knowledge that helped me heal from the inside, out.

Not only did that happen, but so much more. From the birth of my beautiful son to the birth of my coaching business, Havening and self-reflection helped to propel me forward. I learned how to take the experiences of the past, create miraculous possibilities for my future and slow down the hands of time to enjoy each day of my life.

Slowing down was the key.

>> *No matter your story, are you ready to slow your life down and rewrite your future?*

INTRODUCTION

THE ART OF SLOWING DOWN

"The best way to take care of the future is to take care of the present moment."
—Thich Nhat Hanh

SLOW [slō]
ADJECTIVE
Moving, flowing, proceeding without speed or less usual speed.
(Synonyms) *Slow can also be beautifully described as; Leisurely, moderate, deliberate, steady, easy, relaxed, unrushed, gentle, undemanding, comfortable, ponderous, gradual and progressive*

WHAT IS SLOWING DOWN?

What is *slowing down*? How do we slow down? And why is slowing down so important? These are the questions I have pondered for many years. On my search, I discovered the *art of slow living.* I am happy to share the joys of a simpler and more soulful way of living. This allows us to be more present in our daily lives to focus on what truly matters. In this book, I am using my personal and professional past to tell stories of how each individual can create a brighter future, by slowing down and enjoying each present Moment in more spiritually fulfilling ways that can manifest in all areas of life.

Slowing down doesn't mean to stop living passionately, doing nothing or being "lazy." Instead, it's about releasing and letting go of the hectic life. It's about being fully present in every area of your life to create space to truly appreciate and enjoy the time you have while you are still here. *Slowing down* is the practice of intentional thoughts and aligned actions, preparation, forethought, introspection and reflection. It is creating a daily routine that is not only sustainable but supports you towards living an extraordinary life beyond your wildest dreams.

I lived a hectic, chaotic, spontaneous and impulsive life for many years. Due to addiction and trauma, I didn't know how to take time to appreciate beautiful Moments in my life to understand fully what I did have. I finally learned how to take a step back and start living life at a more conscious level. It allowed me to live a chaos-free life. Living life at a slower pace is now merely a lifestyle choice. Slowing down has impacted the quality of my life in a very positive way. When you maintain a life living in the slow lane, you will experience the following miraculous breakthroughs:

- *Create a state of mind of presence to live a fulfilling life with a purposeful sense of being.*
- *Become timeless, consistent and steady.*
- *Be in the present and nourish your soul to allow you to savor each Moment.*
- *Know how to live intention and deep purpose.*
- *Ease stress, anxiety and create balance.*
- *Build stronger, deeper, more intimate, meaningful and lasting relationships simply by being more present and listening with the heart.*
- *Develop a stronger sense of Self connected to your Sources of inspirations or spirituality with the ability to block out the noise and negative influences that deter you from your true path.*

Life is what we make of it. As I've journeyed through this life, I've learned various ways of living and being that helped me to grow in so many miraculous ways. In this book, I've combined a myriad of sources of inspiration throughout my life – teachings from my ancestors, spiritual teachers, families, parents, ancient ways of spiritualities, gurus and ascended masters. These teachings have helped me, protected me and carried me through troubled times, chaos and interference in my life. I learned that no matter what information you've acquired, or guidance you've received from the Universe, God or Source, it's up to you in the way you integrate these lessons and advice to live your life. Once you realize this, your entire life and future can change for the better. Because, ultimately, you are responsible for your actions.

> *"You had no beginning. You're a piece of that Universal mind of Creation and you must see God inside of you and view yourself as a divine creation in order to access the power in your life." (Pg. 137)*
> **—Wayne Dyer, The Essential Wayne Dyer Collection**

Most people don't know how powerful the hidden influences of our teachers and ancestors are in the lives we are all living. Many problems I have faced stem from my past truths, and I was not utilizing my knowledge and guidance properly at the right time in my life. For many years, I was blocked from the light and inner wisdom of Spirit with the use of drugs, alcohol, addictive behaviors, toxic relationships, old patterns of expression and self-sabotaging ways of coping. The persistent, recurring dialogue which kept coming up for me to the *unsolvable* problems in my life was *life is out of control and unmanageable.* It was an old belief system that I could not get rid of. I didn't know how to and wasn't able to harness the power to change because I kept failing at making the right decisions. During my active addictions in relationships, self-esteem issues, drug use and alcoholism, I was going against my inner guidance systems and the path that God planned for me.

As I gained more insight into my life and had a clearer understanding of what was going on, I began to channel my inner guidance to get back on the right path. I used knowledge from my teachers, as well as inspirations from modern-day gurus to design an effective curriculum for living slowly that I still practice daily. I will describe the steps and the tools I gained on my journey to achieve this wholeness.

The spiritual experience, along with the ability to empower humanity through, allowed me to be confident and courageous. The desire to help others using my life story became my passion and drive.

As I traveled along in my journey, I recognized more people were becoming more open to different forms of spiritual practices – which to me, in essence, is genuinely Love and Freedom. It's the freedom to connect to life, to that inner source of Love, peace, joy and wisdom. It's learning how to connect with the power of our teachers and ancestors that came before us. This helps guide us either on the physical plane or spiritual realm. This deeper understanding helped protect me through my most challenging and darkest of times. Through healing myself, I was able to connect deeper with my family and friends in more healthy relationship dynamics. And ultimately, I was able to connect more deeply with society at large to be more in tune as a member of this world as well as be more of service to others.

> *"Life is short. Time is fleeting. Uncover the True Nature. Purify the mind and heart to attain happiness. Be kind; be compassionate. Be generous; do good. Concentrate. Understand. Awaken."* —**Heart of a Buddha, The Amitabha Buddhist Society (Pg. 10)**

I am now conducting workshops and knowledge-sharing sessions to teach people how to establish a relationship with themselves through self-care and self-love and to have them also turn to their friends, guidance, helpers and allies in life for help. Life flows so much more gracefully when we allow our inner guidance to lead the way, aligned with our responsibility for actions. I now live in a realm of higher consciousness, and today possess some psychic and healing abilities, just as many of you do or will, too, once you have done that true healing self-work and learn how to tune in to your Sources. I am a healer, as I have healed myself from the depths of despair and hopelessness. I have found the secret to help women, men and children through connecting to our Higher Selves, through guidance from my Higher Power and the Sources that have kept me healthy all these years.

My relationships and connections to my ancestors, spirit guides, gurus and teachers have strengthened through my use of their teachings. These relationships can be increased or weakened, depending on how you manage your daily actions. For so long, I frantically lived my life in the fast lane, and I channeled into so many confusing frequencies at the same time and became like a lost ship at sea without a compass and anchor. It was so crucial for me to practice slowing down to keep my spiritual connection with my teachers and spiritual guides alive. Through them, I continue to connect to the highest spiritual knowledge at the highest level of consciousness and frequency--connecting me to Source – a God-conscious higher energy and wisdom that continues to guide my life today. These teachers are here to support and guide us, to help us move through challenging obstacles in the way, to protect and watch over us. With this source and guidance, I intuitively feel trust and know it is through love and care. Learning how to strengthen the bond takes continual commitment and daily practice.

I've been lucky enough to learn how to channel my inner guidance on my journey through meditation. We are a part of a beautiful symphony of life, each one singing to our beautiful individual tone in this magical orchestra with our language and frequency. Each one of these teachers has their unique way of teaching and style that will speak to your heart. I've learned the different languages of the heart that spoke to me throughout my life. Each teacher and inspirational leader expressed their style to me through the soul, intuition, heart language, thoughts, values and traditions. I always made an effort to relearn the words of the different teachers.

I also connected to my Divine energy through sacred dance as well. Dance is a way of communicating with all that is. It is a form of communication with mother earth and our teachers. I dug deep to find it and got grounded with this practice. Each species communicates with each other by dancing patterns on the ground. Historically, Indigenous and Native Peoples of the world also used dance as a form of sacred practice that continues to this day. As I researched more into our ancestral backgrounds, the foundation was based on the sacred geometry and sacred sounds of the earth. When we chant a particular sound over sand, the particles will arrange themselves in beautiful geometrical patterns, like the patterns of our dances express our frequency of light that we radiate in our collective Universe. Each one is unique and beautiful. It goes the same for music and visual art, which also creates optical energy. Songs of the heart connect us to our ancestors as well. I grew up listening to Beethoven, Bach and African drums and instruments.

I played the clarinet in marching band for five years and loved the beats of the drums and vibrations as the musical instruments hummed. Music changes something within us and can put us in touch with our inner self. Music is a divine force of sound with power and frequency. Music frequency and vibrations creates a significant effect on the Universe and affects our reality. The practice of sound healing through healing frequencies, created by different sound bowls and instruments, has been so positively widespread and uplifting.

Reflecting back, I can say now that there have been no disappointments in my life; only great lessons that have been taught by great masters revealed through trial and error and time. Each one of the spiritual experiences has been valid as they have taught me to love myself more and more each day and have given me the peace I've been searching for in my life. They all led me back within myself to arrive home where I needed to be, and finally am.

Here are a few of my teachers, gurus, spiritual teachers, and inspirations throughout life that have helped me along the way. Whether it be through an inspirational quote or teaching, each one of these examples served as pathways to spiritual healing for me, and now I am offering them to you as well. Working through illness, dis-ease and imbalance from different angles in my life, each one has been used to help me spiritually heal and bring harmony back. They helped reinforce my whole body, heart and mind – to ultimately nurture my soul back to good health and higher consciousness.

Some of my Inspirations and Influences:

- *Taoism | Buddhism | Christian beliefs*
- *Buddha | Jesus Christ | Dalai Lama*
- *Napoleon Hill | Albert Einstein*
- *Mother Teresa | Mahatma Gandhi | Yogananda*
- *Oprah |Tony Robbins | Martin Luther King, Jr.*
- *Marie Forleo | Gabby Bernstein | Brene Brown*
- *Steve Jobs | Muhammed Ali | Kobe Bryant*

In my personal experience, Taoism has taught me to live gracefully and explore my infinite potential. It helped me walk through my midlife crisis, taught me meditation, social justice and how to practice healthy living. There have been so many positively uplifting lessons through practicing this spiritual philosophy. My goal is to share this knowledge with others and help make this world a better place by living these teachings.

"Live quietly in the Moment and see the beauty of all before you. The future will take care of itself." —**Paramhansa Yogonanda, Autobiography of a Yogi**

Simply translated, here are my three interpretations of the Tao:

1. Way, path, meditative living and even the slowness of the Universe in perfect yin yang balance.
2. Each unknown element that we face in life is in natural order and perfect timing.
3. The Harmonious balance of the Universe in connection to Nature and all that is.

For me, living in the Tao lifestyle is dedicated to living in the presence of the best version of myself. I am living in the flow of life, embracing the rhythm and not allowing outside stories to limit my potential. I learned how to be healthy, flexible and adapt to the changing tides of life, much like a tree that has matured to grow deeper roots to the ground to the earth. I finally learned to be an active and conscious participant in my life with all its richness, as well as have real accountability for my future. It has helped me to cultivate more resilient and robust skills to navigate through the challenges of my life to reap joyful rewards.

I grew up as a Buddhist, practicing the beautiful Buddhist philosophy. Buddhism is a state of lasting, unconditional happiness known as enlightenment. Through this process, I studied the law of cause and effect using practical tools like meditation to gain insight, develop compassion and wisdom. It is the path of spiritual development towards true nature of reality. Meditation practices allow you to change yourself to develop qualities of awareness, kindness, compassion and wisdom. As an enlightened being, you can see the nature of reality clearly and live with that vision. With higher consciousness, Buddhism encourages us all to treat one another with greater understanding, kindness and compassion because nothing is permanent, and change within life and us all is possible.

Buddhism explains cycles of death and rebirth called "samsara." Through building positive karma in kind actions, positive thoughts and good deeds, a Soul will reincarnate many lifetimes while learning many lessons that eventually elicit changes and ultimately enlightenment. The hope is to finally earn our heavenly merits and Soul wisdom to escape samsara and achieve nirvana, an end to all suffering. The understanding of impermanence is at the central core of Buddhism. It helps alleviate pain, as "this too shall pass," and our stories will change. In this way, we do not get stuck as prisoners of our suffering.

This book was written to introduce you to the transformational power of healing change through slowing down – a beautiful and holistic approach to self-awareness, self-improvement and self-healing. I took a deep introspective dive into my own life to discover a more balanced, life-affirming meaningful way of living to reach my own attainable, peaceful nirvana without cycles of trauma and abuse.

In the following chapters, I will share with you techniques to help you slow down, live peacefully, operate at peak performance, achieve optimum health and unlock your highest potential. The methods, meditations, prayers, affirmations and stories here are meant to lift your spirit, enlighten you and inspire you. I will give you access to the same extraordinary knowledge, higher states of awareness, positive mental shifts and skills once achieved by great leaders, yogis, gurus and elite athletes. This list also includes ascended masters and spiritual warriors who have grown through years of learning, training and personal experience.

I have poured years of experience and insights into this transformative handbook, giving you the ultimate tools you will need to experience the profound benefits of slowing down your life immediately. I will also fill you in on best practices, breakthroughs and latest scientific discoveries to allow you to uncover hidden potentials to create an extraordinary life you love. This manuscript is a testimony of how an individual can turn a hectic, once reckless life to one that is peaceful and serene.

This book takes an introspective look into finding your best Self during the most unsettled times.

If you are new but open to the concept of living slowly, I can help shorten the learning curve, save you time and energy and help you create the best foundation for potent and mindful slowing down practices. If you are a seasoned meditation master, powerful breath worker or spiritual advisor, I can help you deepen and broaden your practice. This book will help add knowledge so you can take your life and your work to the next level of self-love and self-care.

The techniques I teach in this book are inspired by ancient teachings, as mentioned from Taoism and Buddhism, as well as a blend from modern masters such as Oprah, Tony Robbins and the late Napoleon Hill. They are similar to ones I have shared with more than hundreds of students and clients. These include life students, corporate executives, coaches, fitness trainers, active duty and retired veterans, Olympic athletes, holistic healers, spiritual teachers and seekers – for more than 20 years.

Like my clients and students, you will feel how gradually slowing down can profoundly change your life and lead to real transformations. The speed in which we move through our lives is in direct correlation and response to stress and challenges, pleasure and pain. In effect, it can make all the difference in the world to our health, mental and emotional well-being, our performance at work, our connections at home and our presence with our loved ones.

Slowing down is a daily practice and becomes an art to help master your life intentionally. Slowing down can be under your control, similar to how breath work helps you calm down and regain yourself, your presence and your focus. This work is an invitation to take part in slowing down your nature and evolve into the person you were meant to become that is present with a higher level of consciousness of your surroundings. There are answers in the speed in which you live that you have probably never observed or explored, and these details are like pathways that can lead to new and profound abilities. Slowing down is a masterful skill set if you want to become not just a high performing individual, but an intentional one enhancing every aspect of your life with more presence and pure joy.

Great masters and gurus in every walk of life know the importance of moving gracefully through life, slowing down, sitting still or meditating and pausing to enjoy every Moment. They realize that the present Moment is the most powerful. In modern times, they have used this tool to relax, decompress, relieve stress and get through critical situations and challenging stressful Moments. All high performers have daily self-care rituals that involve silent meditation, prayer, journaling – all of which require a slower pace and thoughtful existence. It's one of the self-practiced secrets that give them that more bottomless reservoir of endurance, capacity and capabilities, putting them on top of their own active game while keeping them in the slow in a flow state. This quote from the book 1937 by **Napoleon Hill**, *Think and Grow Rich "Whatever your mind can conceive and believe, it can achieve,"* has been a quote that has inspired me along my journey in its use of creating positive energy and the ability of unlocking limitless possibilities with my mind.

One of the most valuable lessons I've learned and is that we have to reach a place of most crucial self-love. If you're reading this now, welcome to the collective global family of spiritual-seeking and awakened beings!

It is time for people from all walks of life to discover, explore and develop the ability to live slowly in "*the Now.*" There is a power in being present and breathing in each Moment. We all need energy, we all give energy and we need to be open to receive it. We all deal with some form of stress and pressure in various ways, and sometimes they are unhealthy for us. The conflict and chaos of today's fast-paced living can feel very challenging and even overwhelming. When you're sitting in a classroom, office, corporate boardroom, on a sales call or an intense situation – grace, poise, focus, clarity, energy and calmness are necessary for these everyday life situations. Living slowly promises these benefits and more; it promises to lead you to self-mastery and transformation in all areas of your life.

"Realize deeply that the present Moment is all you have. Make the NOW the primary focus of your life." —**Eckhart Tolle, The Power of Now: A Guide to Spiritual Enlightment**

WHAT TO EXPECT

"The more that you slow down your life, the more you will fall in love with it each and every day." —**Karen Madewell**

Throughout this book, I will be sharing various ways to slow down – tools, techniques, affirmations, exercises, methods and meditations that I know will enhance every level of your being and life. I have also included a *"7-Day Guide to Slowing Down"* at the end of the book, highlighting three main categories:

Slow-Care (Mind)
Self-Care (Body)
Soul-Care (Spirit)

Every chapter in this thoughtfully curated book has real-life stories from my own life and from people who have inspired me. Each section will help guide you through specific techniques with simple practices every day to slow down your hectic life. If you're feeling scattered, stressed or uninspired, these methods will do wonders as you gracefully and productively move through your day.

As you practice specific slowing down exercises, you will realize slowing down will help alleviate stress, as it will gently remind you to take care of your mind, body and spirit. Slowing down in our fast-paced world will be a life-long process. It will allow you to process, connect and improve every part of your life and help raise positive vibrations.

I will also be introducing the concept of the ***H.O.L.Y. Moments©*** within the book. This is an concept I developed to allow you to experience the miracles in your life as you build awareness in the four types of ***H.O.L.Y Moments©.*** These four types of Moments are defined as ***Holistic, Organic, Little***, and ***Yearned*** Moments in our lives. Recognizing the kind of Moment you have will allow you to appreciate these Moments for what they are as you journey through your life. These Moments may offer you a breakthrough or insights into your life as you are experiencing them. I have experienced many ***H.O.L.Y. Moments©*** on my journey and have embraced the miracles from these Moments. Now I can apply what I've experienced as well as relate to these Moments in my life. I'm excited to share my story in hopes that you will take the time to slow down, appreciate your life. Create happiness, joy and love every day from this point forward!

Lastly, I suggest that you start a personal journal to jot down every ***H.O.L.Y. Moment***© that you mindfully experience throughout your day. Journaling helps you meet your goals and will improve the quality of your life. It can help you clear your head, connect essential thoughts, feelings and behaviors that affect your wellbeing as well as mental health. Write down your favorite "slowing down" ***H.O.L.Y. Moment***© and what you are committed to practicing. Keep a record of your experiences and results. This is a great way to self-reflect to see what's working or not working in your life. This journal will be especially helpful for the **Seven (7) Day *"Guide to Slow Living"*** in chapter 10. Enjoy each Moment and the pace of your daily journey as you get to experience it, as I have done on mine.

*Enjoy each **H.O.L.Y.** Moment on your beautiful journey!*

PART ONE

WHO YOU THOUGHT YOU WERE

THE POWER OF KNOWING YOURSELF

"Nature does not hurry, yet everything is accomplished."
—Lao Tzu

Sometimes, I watch as people slowly turn their heads as I walk by. I often forget that my tattoos speak a language that is only known to me – a secret string of syllables and words that some may think says, "Stay away!" but actually proclaims, "*I survived that too.*" I've sat in the tattoo chair over two dozen times. With each prick of the needle, it was either the beginning of a painful Moment or the closure of another. I have marked my body with intention – both to remember and to let go.

The Universe has given me signs all throughout my life. Sometimes, I look at my precious son and say, "Noah! *Did you feel that?*" The Universe always has something to say or to emote. In those quiet Moments, I truly think it's our intuition and inner guidance that help us move forward. Whether to you it is energy, or God, the Universe, karma or Buddha, it is raw and real – spectacularly aligned to help mold us into something far greater than we could have ever imagined.

Think of this book as my tattoo, something that's shareable in its own language. This book was born from nonsensical chaos – the sheer want to get every important element and learning down on paper to pass to my son as well as my clients. It didn't turn out anything like I first imagined. Instead, with every rewrite and answered question, it shed its skin and ego to help me realize the following valuable truths that I didn't know were deep inside:

- *I have embodied both joy and pain.*
- *My heartbreak gave me purpose.*
- *My body is a canvas much like my future: I own the outcomes.*
- *Recovery has no destination, no one is ever the same as they were before. I am better, more purposeful and deeper in my understanding of the "Why's".*
- *Progress is not about perfection.*

- *Each one of us has glorious attributes we don't even know exist. Only growth from reflection can uncover what's deeper than we may realize.*
- *Slow down and everything you are chasing will come to you.*

I wrote this book for those who have suffered, or are suffering now - living a hectic, chaotic, stressful life and want to make a dramatic change. It doesn't matter where you are in life, there's always a reason to grow UP – not sideways, or down. While I feel like a teacher on some days, on most of my days, I'm forever the student.

My friend and mentor, Kristi, who I call my "*Forever sponsor*", along with so many teachers on my journey, have helped me walk through fire, simply by answering the phone and genuinely being there. I will be forever grateful to this lovely soul whose recovery has been a true blessing in my life. She calls me "*Sweetheart*" and that's what I call others in my life who I adore.

So, join me, *Sweethearts!* Let's explore what happens when hard reflection meets your destiny: *Are you ready to slow down and explore each spectacular Moment?*

TRINH HUYNH ĐINH TRAN
21 - 10 - 1977
BOAT: DN 0750

CHAPTER ONE

STARTING AT GO!...

"Slow down, you're doing fine. You can't be everything you want to be before your time." —**Billy Joel**

You are not your past – you are what you decide to be. Let this be the start of an incredible journey...

Let's revisit my childhood more in-depth. I was born in Vietnam in 1977, the year Apple incorporated, the original Star Wars movie was released and Led Zeppelin and Elvis Presley played their last U.S. concerts. Reggie Jackson also hit three home runs leading the New York Yankees to win the World Series against the Dodgers that year. From the American perspective, it was one hell of a significant year in history, I would say!

The Vietnam War had ended several years prior, but the country was in chaos. The US troops withdrew from Vietnam on April 30th, 1975, on the "*Fall of Saigon*". Due to the unlivable downturn of the economy and a deadly totalitarian regime, my family was forced to flee our homeland for freedom. I was only a year old when my teenage parents and I left the country in June 1979 by boat out into the dangers of the unknown seas. As refugees, we risked our lives and everything we have just for a chance at survival in a new life.

The only escape route was by sea. We trudged through muddy swamps, battled high tide, submerged underwater, and after several failed attempts, our fragile fishing boat set sail on a voyage across the Pacific Ocean. Forty-one courageous human lives were crammed and hidden beneath the deck, holding our breaths – anxious, fearful and more hopeless by the day. We battled dangers of not only the treacherous stormy weather, but dehydration, starvation, siege by Thai pirates seizing, raiding and raping those in our boat.

We finally reached land on the seventh day. We were among one of the very few fortunate boats that arrived at its destination in Indonesia out of the thousands of boats that fled our country. Many starved or died at sea. Many were raided and murdered. We were the lucky ones. It was a devastating, desperate time of life and death for the Vietnamese people. We luckily found safe refuge in an Indonesian refugee camp – Camp Kuku – for almost one year.

Over one million refugees did not make it, and many of those that did faced danger and peril from the pirates. With overcrowded leaking boats crippled in the middle of the vast sea, most went underwater. Lifeless bodies washed up to shore. Parents searched for their missing children. Orphans were being abandoned by parents. Pirates of surrounding countries ransacked many boats, including ours. Women were mercilessly raped, with their men witnessing this. Every single person had to fight for the will to live.

My family, as well as others, was stopped by Thai pirates. They did not rescue us - they robbed us, leaving us stranded and hopeless in the middle of the ocean. I was taken and held captive by the pirates for a short time. Only by God's mercy, was I safely returned to my parents. My parents told me later that a school teacher on the boat, who spoke Thai, begged for my return back to the boat where my parents were anxiously waiting. I am forever grateful to this teacher who saved my life. One Moment I was in my parents' arms and another Moment I was gone. At that time, we could all quickly disappear amid all this chaos called life. In that Moment, I learned that all of *life* is impermanent.

My heart broke after hearing these stories from my parents, but it has solidified my path, has made me stronger and given me an abundance of gratitude in my heart.

The Universe may give us many lessons to overcome, but it also has big and grand plans for us all. The blessings always come after the great lessons of life.

OUR NEW HOMELAND

"Our own life has to be our message."
—Thich Nhat Hanh

My grandmother had already made her way through the immigration process, safely arriving in America. Her journey to the U.S. was not an easy one. She was forced to leave against her will on the *"Fall of Saigon"* on April 30th, 1975, as the U.S. troops were ordered to evacuate Vietnam immediately.

During the pandemonium, my grandmother was pushed into the U.S. helicopter that was in Saigon on a mission delivering food called *"Food for the Hungry."* As the helicopter left the area, her children were left stranded behind to fend for themselves. That day marked the end of the longest war in American history – over nineteen years. *Yet it also marked the beginning of an incredible journey of survival for our family, like so many other families.* Thousands of similar stories were told of families being devastatingly disbanded and separated from loved ones, parents and children during wartime. This war tore our homeland apart and left generational traumas.

By April 1980, faith granted our greatest wish. God did his work and a connection was made with my grandmother. While we were in the refugee camp, the sponsorship process began. Our family was one of the lucky ones. We were hopeful to be on our way to a new life. After arriving in the U.S., we settled in Orange County, where we have lived for the past 40 years.

My story is about growing up in a blue-collar immigrant home in a gang-infested area in Southern California. I grew up with two younger siblings whom I often helped care for. For my parents, transitioning to life in the United States and assimilating into American culture was not easy, especially with the language barriers. My parents, even with their many limitations, demonstrated true resilience, while still being able to provide and feed their family without fail.

In the early 90's while I was in high school, my Mom became a clothing pattern maker and designer who worked directly with the owner of a well-known worldwide skateboard company called Vision Street Wear. Mom impressively created fashion that trended throughout the world.

Growing up with a creative mother, we girls naturally wore clothes that made us stand out from other teenage Asian girls. We learned how to tailor our wardrobe with skater patches and labels. We became fashionably creative with whatever we found in drawers from Mom's projects. At an early age, my sisters and I broke away from the "*traditional Vietnamese Asian teenager*". Having a trendy Mom, we were supported as well as inspired by her passion to re-define the Asian-American culture by sporting a famous streetwear brand with wild hair, visible tattoos and piercings at a young age. We had more rebellious freedom in how we looked than the typical Asians from more conventional families because of Mom's career. Later in life, this ended up playing a part in our identities, expressions, who we became, the friends we hung out with and how we integrated into American society.

On the outside, our family looked relatively healthy. However, at the same time behind closed doors, Mom suffered grief and depression. I believe this was largely due to the unhealed traumas she experienced during the war, as well as being separated thousands of miles away from her homeland. I always felt there was something severely wrong at home. Mom never seemed happy, but she also never talked about her fears, loneliness or suffering. I don't blame her. She always remained strong. I can only imagine that she suffered significant trauma from the war and post-traumatic stress of being forced out of her homeland, 2,000 miles away from her parents and extended family.

My relationship and connection with my father was especially tricky. We hardly saw or communicated with him. I resented him and my mother for years because I felt, as a family unit, we could have been stronger if we learned how to connect and understand the pain we were all enduring on the inside. He wasn't a bad father. He just was a very hard worker dealing with the pressures of survival and providing for us. Dad hustled and did the best he could. Both my parents did the best they could. His routine of leaving at 4:00 am trekking to Los Angeles and operating a city bus all day long was a daily routine, working 6-7 days a week at times. He was never home and would arrive home after a long shift, after our homework was done and problems had already been resolved. We were already in bed before we saw him. I feel like he missed out on some crucial years and crucial parts of our lives when we needed him the most. We especially yearned for the emotional care, nurturing and protection that we required from a male figure within a family.

We ultimately learned how to take care of ourselves. I personally felt abandoned and alone all the time.

Growing up, I didn't feel like I fit in. My family didn't know how to give me the love I needed and deeply desired. I wanted that perfect type of familial love I watched on Disney movies and television. I don't remember feeling the warmth of a hug, kisses and closeness that a young child needs in their formative years. I always felt as if I didn't have anyone to care for my emotional well-being. I had to take care of myself. I sought shelter in the arms of the wrong boys, and then men.

I kept myself warm and when I needed more fire, I unfortunately, looked for it in all the worse places.

My parents were young and traumatized teenagers when they had me. I used to fault them for so much, but as I grew and learned that while I missed their hugs, my parents only gave me what they were capable of at the time. For so long, I was angry at them. I didn't recognize how hard it is for someone to flee a war-torn country being children themselves with young children to raise until I became an adult. Knowing what I know today, I probably wouldn't have rebelled so severely, but I was also a child coping in the best ways I could in my circumstances.

THE MAGIC "SPEED UP" PILL

"The world belongs to the energetic."
—Ralph Waldo Emerson

Despite the emotional deficits in my life, things were somewhat normal until I was thirteen years old. During a basketball game, I had a significant accident dislocating my right kneecap as I came down from a rebound and had to have major surgery to reattach the ligaments. I wound up in a cast for six months, became immobile, developed atrophy and coped by binging on food. I developed an eating disorder that led to severe body image issues. Desperate to lose weight, I turned to dangerous weight loss pills prescribed by a physician and got hooked on them at the tender age of thirteen.

It was a bad situation. I was only a child when I got the prescription for Phentermine (Phen Phen). This prescription didn't come with a medical plan, nor was I being monitored under a physician's care. There was no life instruction manual. I was too young to know how to incorporate this drug into my life. I was also not armed with the knowledge of proper nutrition and exercise that I have today. Looking back, I don't blame myself anymore for this bad habit I developed.

The bottle said, "*Take as needed,*" and I took them "as needed" to feel better for everything. Feelings of being overweight, tired, lonely, happy, sad, discontented, depressed, angry, the list goes on. The use of pills became a daily "*thing*" to help ease whatever was going on inside me. This habit became a big secret I couldn't tell anyone. Eventually my emotions were all over the place. The shame of being frowned on for being drug-dependent kept me in a reckless cycle of silence.

My abuse with this dangerous pill lasted for over six years. The "*Magic pill*" acted as a stimulant to stay awake and sharpen my focus so I could do homework. The result was perfect each time. I used them whenever I needed a boost. Thinking back, this jolt of energy magically felt like drinking smooth and robust coffee, only better, faster and easier to hide.

Unfortunately, in the late 1990s, the FDA recalled the pills because of all the complaints and health concerns from patients. The pills were prescribed to anyone complaining about weight issues. However, there were given without a safety warning about the addictive nature of them or the dangerous effects it would cause. My symptoms included a rapid and irregular heartbeat, insomnia, sweaty palms, anxiety, attention deficit, nervousness and lack of concentration.

I didn't know how much danger I was in until years later. It was too late, because I had grown addicted to the effects of the chemicals. Even though I was experiencing side effects and symptoms, it did not stop me from searching for more. When the supply ran out, I stole the remaining pills from my mother's medicine cabinet. Eventually I found out I could order a similar type of pill on the internet or buy them in Mexico, or wherever I could get them by forging prescriptions. The availability of pills caused me to prolong their use. I didn't understand what was going on in my mind and turned into a full-blown "*druggie*". I didn't know stopping was an option. My body's dependency couldn't rationalize the possibility I could stop. I didn't even know I had a problem.

My addiction got to the point where I was using all kinds of pills in social settings and even in secrecy. I took them wherever I could. At school, work, vacation, parties, visiting relatives, cruise ships – everywhere I went. The symptoms got worse. I began to make more unfortunate decisions.

I felt so lost and became a lost girl.

Looking back, I am glad these performance enhancement, appetite-suppressing obesity drugs got banned because of the effects they had on my heart and my life. I am sure it could have been fatal with continued use. *I escaped a possible death?* I write this in my story in hopes health care providers and physicians do not irresponsibly write prescriptions for potent drugs to children and troubled teens without any warnings to family and subsequent follow-ups with teens. My hope is to share this to help empower others to not rely on dangerously destructive drugs to self-medicate and numb out emotional pain from life events.

THE AWAKENING

"Turn your wounds into wisdom."
—Oprah Winfrey

The traumatic event of being sexually attacked and raped I described at the beginning of this book happened to me at the age of fifteen. This terrible incident forced me to go into survival mode. I lived with the painfully shameful secret for a lot of years. It slowly poisoned me from the inside-out. It brought my defenses up to shut out the trauma and pain that was infecting me on the inside so no one could see the flaws and suffering. This event desensitized me and forced me to dramatize my life in grown-up situations with recurring flashbacks of the trauma as a teenager. To make matters worse, my secret pill habit was also killing me from the inside out.

I was no longer a lost girl, but I was simply going to be nowhere to be found. I will never let you in, and you will never really know who I am.

For years, I couldn't even remember what happened to me because I buried this memory deep in the past. All I could recall and the story I told myself was that I was *"picked up"* while waiting at a bus stop early in the morning, driven off and attacked in a deserted orange grove only a city away. I couldn't remember the details of that day. I really never told anyone what happened because of the shame of skipping school that day. It was only recently that I started speaking about how being assaulted forever changed my life. I did a lot of trauma work with counselors, therapists, gurus and spiritual guides. The most helpful was the deep self-reflection work I did in recovery and several coaching programs as an adult.

What happened? What was the real story? What have I been telling myself all these years and why?

*D*uring high school, in my sophomore year, I was thoroughly entrenched and in love with a Vietnamese boy that was freshly released from jail. I labeled him my "*boyfriend*" for almost six months. One day, I made a terrible decision to ditch school to see this boyfriend who was on house arrest at his apartment in Huntington Beach, where he lived with his Dad. My parents didn't like him to say the least. He was tall, good looking, had a charming personality and a bad boy vibe. He was emotionally and physically exciting, but risky. I didn't know he was not the right person for me. We were young and in love. That's all that mattered. I was always attracted to bad boys, especially the emotionally broken ones. The ones I felt needed rescuing – whom I could help feel better, and in return, they would comfort me. The type of boys I saw in movies that were portrayed as the adventurous hero promising a happy ending. My knight in shining armor that came in to rescue me and save the day.

I always had the urge to rebel against my parents. Forbidding me and keeping me away from something, made me want more of it. I desired a secret and forbidden love full of passion, intimacy and a sense of safety. Something I didn't see my parents consistently show each other. *Maybe my parents always screamed and yelled at each other was because they were lacking this? Perhaps that is why they abused one another?* Or was it because of something *profound at an even deeper level,* like old traumas and the baggage of poverty, war and immigrant struggles? With endless hours of laboring and work, compounded with limited time and resources for healing and self-care, my parents' broken expressions of love were most likely a by-product of years of hurt they endured.

Traumas and pain perpetuate and manifest different cycles. My family was no different from this painful and truthful reality. Maybe that's why I turned out the way I did. In great frustration and in their internal struggles with the external life, Mom and Dad argued all the time. Mom would cope by using abusive language and demeaning language. Dad would cope and still copes, by smoking.

My childhood home often felt like a war zone, where I did not feel emotionally safe or stable. I internalized that trauma and pain. I didn't feel the peace and joy of a quiet, loving home. There was so much anger and resentment. Mom told us that she got the short end of the stick by marrying my father, who didn't provide her luxuries promised by other men back in Vietnam as a teenager. Dad had a hard life too. His mother was forced to leave Vietnam and left him an orphan as his father had passed years prior. My Dad really never shared stories about his father, my grandfather. This is probably why I never ask about people's lives and how they grew up. I never really felt I had one of my own, except for what had personally happened to me. It is not that I'm disinterested in others, but it is more the lack of experience I had with my own ancestors sharing their pasts through storytelling with me. I know my father grew up the best way he could without parental support and love. He raised us the best he could with the tools he had. Both my parents did.

Witnessing all this emotional detachment and deep wounds, I became desperate and addicted to the feeling of being loved and cared for. I was yearning to have someone embrace me, save me and rescue me. Maybe that is why I gravitated towards my bad-boy boyfriend. I felt the need to see him all the time. He protected me from my parents' anger towards each other. He shielded me from the feelings of abandonment and not receiving the love I needed from my family of origin. His voice was sweet and loving. He called me by my Vietnamese name, *Thy*.

Did I make a mistake in going against my parents' wishes to continue seeing this boy? I have always wondered. He was a bad influence, but he felt emotionally safe for me. He was physically safe as well. I don't remember being hurt or harmed by him in any way. He was a bad boy and made some bad choices that got him arrested and in trouble with his gang. He was on house arrest for burglary or some sort of crime. I don't remember exactly what he went in for; I don't think I ever asked. I blindly pursued this connection of youthful passion. Honestly, I didn't care about any of that. A man loved me, and that was all that mattered at that time. I never asked about his life or got to know him. This is a trend that stayed with me for years with all future men that I got involved with – emotionally, physically, and spiritually dangerous men. I ran my life based on intuition and what I knew about them from what they chose to tell me.

Maybe I was too scared to see the truth about people?

I never really understood what I had gotten myself into when I met him. I never asked questions. But somehow, intuitively, I still almost had the psychic ability to know what was going to happen next. I trusted the Universe, yet blindly without more in-depth understanding. I didn't know how to describe what was in my heart and around me.

On the cold morning of the *Awakening*, I couldn't predict what was going to happen. No one ever can. I recall opening my eyes to a new day and was on a mission to ditch school to see that boy. It was the perfect plan. I was going to take a bus to Huntington Beach and he was going to walk to the 711 down the street to greet me. It was all going to happen and it was going to be great. We were going to see each other, make love and spend time together. Before school got out, I would take a bus back home and no one would find out. I was young, in love, rebellious and ran towards a forbidden love.

It was a no-fail plan. We had it all planned out. I was adamant not to be discovered as a bad daughter. I remember slowly walking into my Mom's room, tapping her on the shoulder, whispering goodbye to her. I told her I was going to walk to school for band practice. I remember pretending to be a well-behaved, young, independent and responsible person that didn't want to bother her sleep. Since it was so early in the morning, I knew she would have refused to take me to school anyway.

Honestly, I can't even remember my footsteps leaving the house. I can't recall arriving at the bus stop, or looking at a bus schedule or sitting down waiting for a bus. The foggy winter morning weather was cold, dark and grey. I remember a lowered dark Nissan vehicle with tinted windows pulling up to the curb as I waited on the bus stop bench. The door swung open, he asked if I would like a ride and I excitedly hopped in the car without question or hesitation. The door shut behind me. I took one glance at this older man in his 40's and in my gut, I felt something was very wrong. There was a fear that loomed over me. I knew it was fear because I couldn't even look straight into his eyes or even look towards the driver seat. I just know I didn't want to get to know him.

This memory reminds me of the victimhood mentality I had growing up. I was a sweet innocent girl that needed someone to rescue me because I needed a ride. Hoping the person in the car was a kind person, willing to help me with a ride as I waited at the bus stop so early in the morning.

At that Moment, it felt like an out of body experience. I just knew I wasn't meant to be there. Now, I know my body was destined to go through the physical trauma so I could learn the valuable life lessons I know today. Very similar to how over hundreds of life lessons and out-of-body experiences helped me to understand the experience of being somewhere I was not supposed to be. I felt like my soul was outside of my body watching over me. Almost like I was under God's protection. I knew that ditching school was wrong. Everything was wrong about that morning, and there was no escaping the inevitability of what was to come.

During the car ride, I panicked for a bit but managed to calm myself, hoping the end of this horrible movie would end soon. Minutes later, he pulled into the gas station on Fairview and Haster Street. He jumped out and ran in to buy something. I remember yanking on the door handle to get out, but the door was locked. I never considered that the child lock was on. That could have been a possibility, but everything moved so quickly that it was all a blur. The man rushed back into the car and started driving. I sat there quietly, holding my breath in fear.

To this very day, I can still feel that gut-wrenching sense of fear.

My boyfriend lived westbound off the 22 in Huntington Beach. When the driver pulled the car onto the road again, he entered 22 Eastbound. My stomach dropped. The car was going in the wrong direction. I knew there was danger headed my way. I felt something terrible was going to happen.

When we arrived at the empty orange groves, I can't remember much except the morning air was crisp with the scent of tangerine with the leaves billowing, eerily back and forth. I didn't say a word the entire time. I remember feeling scared, disappointed and unsafe. I also remember the feeling of being frustrated and disappointed with myself as I made a decision that went against my intuition.

As he drove slowly through the orange groves and came to a stop, he told me to get out of the car to go to towards the back of the car. He ordered me to go to the back seat, yanked my pants down, and pushed me over the back seat. He forcibly entered and began to rape me. All I can remember was looking forward and then to the side towards the steering wheel. There were moments I closed my eyes and imagining this was not happening. I was too afraid to turn and look at him. He pulled my hair and told me to shut my mouth. While being sexually attacked by this monster, all I kept thinking to myself was how I was going to explain this to my boyfriend who I'm sure was feverishly waiting for me?

After it was all done, I remember pulling my pants up and was told to get back into the passenger seat. He started the car, backed out of the groves, jumped on the freeway and after a 10-minute drive, dropped me off. I don't remember where he dumped me, but it was nowhere near Huntington Beach. Somehow in the haze of it all with a sense of urgency, I still managed to make my way to my boyfriend's house. I remember desperately wanting to tell him what happened, but couldn't bear the truth.

What was I going to tell my boyfriend? What was I going to say? I hitchhiked and this is was what happened today?

I recklessly hitched a ride to get to my lover's house without thinking of the risks and got sexually attacked. I've hitch hiked before, in broad daylight with friends, but this time it was terrible and different. This time, I was alone, vulnerable and he wasn't there to rescue me. I couldn't bear the burden of hurting him as I was hurting myself. I refused sex that day. I left his house before school got out and I managed to get home.

Life was a blur from that point on.

I never waited for someone to rescue me ever again – a trait I've held on to all my life. I have had this similar reckless behavioral pattern for years. More than ever before, I moved around in life based on desire and blind faith alone – no intentional planning, waiting and anticipating for anyone. I left relationships, abandoned relationships and situations easily if I didn't feel safe.

The most terrible memory association was the smell of alcohol. When I came home to wash myself up in the bathtub I smelled alcohol coming from my vagina. This man had been drinking alcohol before he picked me up from the bus stop. This made me feel sick to my stomach. This monster violated me and sexually attacked me while he was inebriated. I desperately tried to wash any traces of my rapist from within me. Sadly, sex was never the same with men in the future and anything that had to do with sex repulsed me. From that point on I would never have a natural orgasm with a man without thoughts of being raped or violent fantasies. It took me a long time to even look into a man's eyes. I was never able to let myself be free. I was never able to allow myself to love within healthy dynamics. I was in a mental prison trap. I had a lot of secrets and became as sick as my secret. I had many of them that twisted me up within. I was always able to put on a front and say I was "OK" when I was not Ok inside.

Fear of victim-blaming and not having any support, I never told anyone of my hitchhiking, hopping into a stranger's car, being raped against my will and abandoned in a cold and deserted orange grove one city away from home. I fumbled my way home, just as I had fumbled through life with this silent secret. This event changed my life forever. For decades, I kept this trauma a secret and held its poisonous effects within my own body and consciousness without any form of release or relief.

This harrowing incident traumatized me and held me hostage in its shame for many of my teenage years into adulthood. For the next twenty years, I was haunted by it and trudged through a life riddled with fear, shame and guilt. I kept that secret until I turned thirty-nine years old. I was finally ready to tell my story.

My life changed dramatically from that damaging event, and I fell quickly into a victimhood mentality that allowed my life to spiral out of control. Reflecting back and after much deep healing work, I know now I was a broken soul and had the deep need to rescue men. I never wanted my boyfriends to feel abandoned as I did. The codependence dance was on.

I constantly had an intense pull of continuing codependent dynamics into adulthood. Looking back now, I honestly don't remember what exactly happened in my life leading up to the days nor the years after the *Awakening* took place. I blocked this Moment and other Moments in my life easily. My life has been a big blur. There have been so many Moments I felt trapped, alone and helpless. This *Awakening* has especially been hard to describe to anyone.

I always described that incident being a kidnapping. I was still a child and he was an older responsible adult who kidnapped and raped me forcibly against my will. But here is where the guilt and victim-blaming mentality comes in – should I even call it kidnapping when I made the decision to jump in the car? I hitchhiked. *That's what happened.* I chose to hop into a stranger's car without questioning anything at 5:30 in the morning, without asking one single question. I vaguely and quickly explained to this stranger where I needed to go. And he went where he wanted to go. Everyone has their agenda – mine was a naive one; his plan was a sexually violent one. What I do know is that that painful Moment woke me. It shook me to my core and forced me to face myself on so many levels.

I was riddled with so much guilt and shame throughout life. It was easier to cope by blocking out what happened than to confront it or tell anyone. I internalized the trauma and felt like it was my fault. I blocked out the memory so much that I don't even remember what I wore, what I was carrying, how I looked or how I really felt. All I knew was I was on a mission to get to my boyfriend's apartment to get a hit of potent love or whatever it was I needed from him at that time.

I don't remember grabbing my clarinet for the band practice I wasn't going to. I do remember lying to my Mom that I was going to a marching band practice that wasn't happening. It was the perfect excuse. One that my Mom wouldn't have argued with or would ever have found out. It was the perfect plan – because I was right, she never found out I ditched school on that fateful morning until I finally told her what happened decades later in 2018.

My eyes were wide open and my defenses went up. Everyone became a predator to me.

I trusted no one. Not even my family.

I remember trying to tell my Dad when I was in college around 18 or 19 years old. I tried to describe to him what happened to me on that fateful morning. How I was sexually attacked and how there was something desperately wrong with me. Disappointingly, with his inability to not know what to say or how to be supportive, he said whatever has happened to me in my life was from my decisions and "It was my fault." I was his eldest daughter, so I just took responsibility and accepted his words as being my truth. However, it was so hurtful to hear this judgment from my own father. I made the conscious decision to then shut down from every man even further. I thought to myself, if my father couldn't help me through the feelings of brokenness, no one can. *My heart broke for me, and it's been broken all these years, up until recently.* I refer to this sexually violent incident as *"The Awakening"* because it aggressively forced me to awaken healing on so many levels after the suffering and pain.

"Looking back, I'm sure Dad wasn't intentionally trying to hurt me by not listening or showing lack of emotion. He just didn't have the tools to be supportive or know what to say. I don't blame him. Being a parent myself, I can only imagine the pain I put him through knowing your own child was a victim of the cruel world he warned me about all these years. I love and forgive you Dad." —**Journal entry**, *January, 1 2015*

CHAPTER TWO

THE "ISM'S"

"Life is 10 percent what happens to me and 90 percent of how I react to it." —**Charles Swindoll**

What other choice did I have but learn how to shut out trauma and unhealed wounds that were bottled up inside?

As a way to cope, I ended up in spiritually broken, toxic relationships, attracting them wherever I went because I felt broken inside. We tend to attract similar vibrations to the messages we send out to the Universe. We are each other's mirrors. I overcompensated my lack of understanding of the victimhood mentality by entering into and enduring vicious cycles of codependency, workaholism and alcoholism - just about any "*ism*" that you can imagine.

I inevitably ended up in a mentally, psychologically and verbally abusive failed marriage with a man who had a mental illness. Even after my divorce, there followed a string of toxic relationships with broken people who I tried to fix and rescue. I found myself in these relationships over and over again. I believe that it was because I was still not whole and on my road to healing myself from within.

Our most profound and intimate relationships are our most accurate mirrors reflecting what we cannot see within ourselves individually.

In that sense, we are all one another's most excellent teachers through the lessons of life. I had a profound misunderstanding of who I was, what my purpose was in life, and I kept going back to what I thought I deserved. I wore a mask of being a strong woman, daughter, mother and partner for so long. I tried to overcompensate by putting my best effort in to fix others externally and internally. It took me a long time to realize I was worthy of love too. Only when I finally came into full acceptance of who I am was I able to stop the vicious cycle of self-abuse and self-abandonment manifested within broken dynamics and relationships. I finally realized that life is a beautiful flow of reciprocity when it is in perfect balance.

With all the inner emotional turmoil, I found myself taking more and more pills to keep up the façade of being okay. My drug use escalated as my self-worth continued to diminish. I gave little thought to my behavior as being drug abuse. I justified my usage legitimately because I purchased the pills through an authorized distributor with a valid manufacturer name on the bottle. Once in a while, I would have an actual prescription for the pills and that made me feel good. After all, I was not a "*street junkie*" or doing deals in the dark alleys. I was out of control emotionally but was still functioning. I continued to take more pills to get through each day.

My addiction to pills led me to painkillers. I would ask for a prescription in the names of my family members. Suddenly my Mom had "*back pain,*" and my father had "*arthritis,*" and I was under the disguise of being a good daughter getting prescriptions for them. I used painkillers as muscle relaxers. This allowed me to relax after a long day. Despite the drug abuse, I was still a high performer at work. At the age of 16, I began working within call centers as a telemarketer. I always felt on top of life using the illusion of the "*magic pills*" to enhance my performance at work. It also made me feel better about myself and my life because I was able to check out.

When I got to college, I was a full-blown *adrenaline junkie* and continued to move quickly through school. From there, I moved into the fast-paced corporate world. I didn't know stopping or *slowing down was an option*. My body and mind got hooked to the fast lane. What didn't occur to me was that I had become an addict. I justified the pills. I got used to the effects of feeling a jolt of energy. I slowly shifted the way I thought about the pills. I eventually used it to numb out physically, emotionally and spiritually. I used it numb out and not face reality, my traumas or depression. Then one-day alcohol came into the picture again. I acquired the taste of alcohol after high school. I was still repulsed with the smell and taste of alcohol partially from my distant memory of being sexually attacked four years prior. However, once I discovered the effects of alcohol, the dance with alcohol was on. I just used it as another way to numb out. At that point, there was no stopping the melodies and the daily rhythm and dance with the devil.

Since alcohol was easily accessible, I was able to use it almost daily. I had every excuse to drink. I drank during lunch, dinner, weekends, at parties, clubs, bars, with friends and family. Unfortunately, as I entered college, becoming an independent young woman, excessive parties came into the picture and so did the more potent party drugs. I ended up experimenting with MDMA (Molly), ecstasy and even tried crystal methamphetamines during my last year of college to increase the illusions of pleasure and connection. *That was a big mistake.* Meth, along with a lethal combination of alcohol, brought me to my knees. I hit my first rock bottom during this time in my life. My addiction to both drugs and alcohol physically and spiritually broke me. I spiraled downhill fast, but I kept coming back to using it as a way to escape. After the alcohol wore off, I kept hitting the drugs to feel better.

I became more lost and confused than ever.

By the time I was 20, alcohol was everywhere. It turned up at every company event, family gathering, music and art venues. I was addicted to the mind-altering effects and the confidence boost it gave me. I liked the way it made me feel at ease in my skin. The only problem was I didn't know how to control my liquor or to stop after one or two drinks. I would have one too many at every chance, pass out, and wake up hungover from blackouts almost weekly. For several years, I justified my drinking problem as being socially acceptable and that it wasn't a hard party drug, so it should be okay.

But alcohol is a drug. And *addiction is addiction.*

Thankfully, I only used crystal meth for a short period. That combination was the most destructive. I tried to quit drinking alcohol several times on my own but spiraled into years of endless relapses with old toxic patterns when alcohol was in the picture. I had always known that there was something wrong with the way I was using and abusing other things in my life.

I switched addictions – from food to drugs, to alcohol, to men, to chasing people, places and things that gave me instant gratification or a "high."

Everything became a "*Magic Pill.*" I started to experience the "*Phenomenon of Craving,*" that was talked about in the Big Book of Alcoholics Anonymous. For years I felt so wounded, so empty, so emotionally and spiritually unfulfilled.

I will explain more about this inner phenomenon of struggle and craving in the following chapters as I take you through the journey of life in love, business and recovery.

"I have turned my life around and overcome addictions. I aspire to inspire others that they can overcome too."—**Journal entry**, *November 2019*

WORKAHOLISM

"Only put off until tomorrow what you are willing to die having left undone." —**Pablo Picasso**

After years of living life under the influence of one form of addiction to another, workaholism became a problem too. Working a lot was very validating and affirming to an exterior identity that was crumbling within. I climbed my way up the corporate ladder as a recruiter, but still had a highly addictive personality. I even got high from interacting and engaging in social relationships with people.

I was torn between low self-esteem, ego and pride, the highs and lows that come with a great career and the money that came with it too. I couldn't slow down. Money, power, prestige, sex, love and adrenaline-fueled business transactions continued to allure me. Before working as a recruiter, I trained myself by working long hours as a telemarketer. I was able to juggle a significant workload using magical energy pills.

I hit my physical, emotional and spiritual rock bottom during the last year of college. Life was utterly unmanageable. I graduated from college. I had a considerable amount of debt. My credit score went below 400 and my self-esteem went even lower. Self-dignity and self-love were non-existent. I told myself that no one's love was ever enough. I said they broke me, but my truth amounted to *"never being good enough."* I coped with the pain by continuing unhealthy habits.

During several episodes and bouts of depression, I acted on thoughts of suicide by drinking and overdosing on pills, hoping it could be the last escape. I drank until I blacked out and didn't want to wake up. My desire for life itself was gone. I was so powerless at that Moment, so filled with anger, resentment, guilt, self-pity and shame. The walls went up, but I continued to make unhealthy decisions. After almost dying, losing my illusion of normalcy in life, losing friends, family and self-esteem, I knew I had a choice to make. There was no turning back if I kept going in the same direction.

I finally sought help.

I went to therapists, temples, churches and any other place I could find peace and solitude for my broken spirit.

Although my friends and family admired me for my exterior success and my respect at work, the magnitude of my emotional tumble was immeasurably overwhelming. I had to cope with the secrets and lies I was telling myself. I fell from grace and was deeply hurting. I wasn't able to talk about how I felt for a long time. I had such great shame and was embarrassed about the things I had done – for many years, I was inflicted with so much guilt and self-condemnation. I had an obsession of the mind and wasn't able to accept that my life was so out of control.

"I finally hit an extreme inner turmoil and an emotional bottom." **—Journal entry**, *July 15, 2019*

CHAPTER THREE

SOBRIETY FIRST: HEALTH AS A PRIORITY

"Slow down and enjoy life. It's not only the scenery you miss by going too fast – you also miss the sense of where you are going and why." —**Eddie Cantor**

In 2002, I was lucky to reach a turning point. I found Alcoholics Anonymous (AA) through a man I met who was in recovery. I met him while working at a call center staffed with other recovering addicts and alcoholics. We became friends and eventually married. But this marriage was not easy at all. He suffered with mental illness and our family coped through many manic episodes and sleepless nights. The blessings I received from that marriage were I discovered 12-step programs and I had a child named Noah – *my greatest blessing in life.*

This broken and emotionally straining relationship taught me a lot about myself and the world. I survived being with someone who had bipolar manic depression. We had many dealings with police officers, family law courts, restraining orders, mental hospitals, jails and support groups as we lived with his bipolar disease.

Luckily, my son had one stable parent that never had problems with the law. I was never court-mandated to get sober or got in trouble. I'm also happy to report that I have never seen the inside of a police car, jail cell or worse – end up inside a coffin.

I've been lucky on many fronts, but my journey on the road to recovery was not a smooth one. Recovery has been filled with giant boulders and roadblocks filled with immense emotional challenges, obstacles and hurdles to overcome. I trudged through the work daily, fixing the wreckage of tremendous suffering, self-abuse, self-abandonment and cruelty. I have incurred car accidents, financial misfortunes, emotional misguidance, relationship mistreatment, mental illness, health ailments and emotional trauma. Looking on the bright side of things, without the painful climb, I would not be able to experience and appreciate the beauty of life fully today. These Moments of clarity are also characterized as magical "aha-Moments," delightful breakthroughs, nuggets of wisdom, earth's natural elements of love, enlightening spiritual guidance, self-love wins and magical soul-awakening Moments on my road of recovery.

When I walked into my first AA meeting, I knew I would be in danger if I didn't come back. I needed a lot of help. I was desperate. I had the willingness to do whatever it took to feel better. I committed to the program daily to begin the inside healing process. AA helped slow me down physically and mentally, but it was unable to help me address the one single event that had brought me to knees. In the program, I truly learned about acceptance and forgiveness. I learned how not to drink. I learned how to stay away from things that hurt me, but I never learned who I was.

Years later, in 2016, a therapist during a session said something that was very eye-opening. "*What it sounds like to me, the sexual assault reduced your life to one single event in the first year of high school.*" A stunning Moment of realization for me – all I could do was nod. At that Moment, I realized I held onto a secret that had manifested into a toxic belief system that nearly killed me. In the program of recovery, we are told we become as sick as our secrets. And this is *precisely* what happened inside me.

Over the course of 10 years, I had seen many people lose their lives in their addiction and suffer severely, including myself. It was easy to let go of the chemical dependencies, but I still had a lot of inside work to do. Looking back to my drinking and using years, I put myself into risky situations and always found myself on my knees praying to my Higher Power, thanking him that I still had the chance to make my life right again. This was usually after blackouts and coming back to consciousness in the morning. I have had close friends who committed suicide by hanging themselves, others who have overdosed on drugs and others who died in vehicular accidents involving a drunk driver or someone under the influence.

Once I had a boyfriend who almost lost his life after a long night of partying using drugs mixed with alcohol. He fainted on the toilet and jammed his skull into the corner in the bathroom up against a very heavy wooden door. His body blocked the entrance and I had to push the door forcefully to get in. I thought I was going to crush his skull. Barely breathing and turning blue, I sat him up to help him regain consciousness. *What would have happened if I didn't get in there in time? How would I have explained this to the police or our families?* With God's mercy, I had many lessons in life with too many close calls. My decision to choose sobriety over getting loaded became a matter of life or death. So I continued to stay sober and clean, no matter what.

As I was winning at the game of life in 2005, with a flourishing career and the accumulation of material things, my 12-step program stopped working. Deep down, something inside me knew I could quickly rise or fall, just as during the rest of my volatile life. I started having a fear of losing what I had worked so hard to acquire. I was so desperate to stop the voices of fear and insecurity in my head. I continued to cry out in desperation for help. Although I began to start feeling better, I was still very emotionally dependent on people, places and things. Emotional dependency was the worst. I often told myself I was not good enough. I felt like a failure, continuously having setbacks, and my out-of-control mind caused me to feel very insecure. I scrambled and found myself searching for more answers. I discovered there was more than just being sober from drugs and alcohol. I had yet to identify other self-sabotaging patterns and harmful crutches in my life that were controlling my life such as anger, emotional outbursts and negative self-talk. Not recognizing these character defects brought on by deep trauma was slaughtering me from the inside out. I had to dig even deeper within myself. I learned about *Emotional Sobriety*. Without emotional sobriety, it was really hard to eliminate old patterns of behaviors that caused me to drink and use or act out obsessively.

I continued to *work on myself* with the little hope I had left. I had to have *a clear vision* and know what my end-game was going to be. My emotional wounds tormented me and clouded up my goals. I had a hard time moving forward. Up until that point, luckily I didn't do anything majorly destructive in my life to become hospitalized. I never received a psychological diagnosis for any disorder other than depression. Still, for some reason, I swear I could have also have been struggling with bipolar disorder, ADHD and OCD (Obsessive Compulsive Disorder). At times, I was convinced that during some Moments in my life, I was so unstable that I had gone crazy.

A major realization for me was that I continuously surrounded myself with unhealthy people and circumstances. Awareness set in. However, a daunting realization was made.

I was the person that people needed to stay away from.

I was that toxic friend, lover, sister, daughter and partner.

"There was no more running away from accountability and others anymore. I stood there at the doorway of my life and realized how broken I was. Something needed to change…" **—Journal entry**, *November 22, 2017*

THE SLOW CLIMB: OTHER 12-STEP PROGRAMS

"Power is of two kinds: One is obtained by the fear of punishment and the other by acts of love." —**Mahatma Gandhi**

While one problem or another seeped into every crack of my life, life got too overwhelmingly complex. I needed more guidance and more in-depth answers. After a few years of being clean and sober, I saw myself taking back the control. I found myself back in the driver seat navigating my life in new directions. Although AA worked really well, I felt the program was not enough for the healing I still needed to do. I knew there were more layers I needed to address within myself. I opened my heart and allowed my *Souls' Guide* to show me other ways to experience healing and spiritual breakthroughs. I was introduced to various tools to dig deeper so I could bring to light the sources of deeper pain. I had to figure out what was missing and not working in my life. I went deep inside beneath the layers of the psyche – the origins of wounds.

Although I was physically sober from chemicals, I was not very emotionally sober. As I got into one relationship after the next, everything was triggering. I had set sail on a path of self-destruction once again. That was until I joined my knowledge of AA and other self-empowerment programs – particularly a method called *"Havening." Havening* helps to dig deep into the brain to de-traumatize the memory and remove its negative effects from both my psyche and body through self-soothing techniques. *Havening* uses imagination, healing sensory techniques like touch and emotionally comforting your own needs, as tools to help the body and mind process painful and unreconciled memories.

Through *Havening* and self-reflection, I gained an incredible amount of self-awareness through deep healing. I believe there are two fundamental truths that I often overlooked in my everyday life:

First I am human, and am also part of a global community.

Secondly, as Buddha puts it much more eloquently – all humans suffer.

I often forget that simply *being* is the root and the exact purpose of our existence. We are human *beings*, after all, and are the source behind all the *doing* we've relied on to help define our place and pace in the world. Yet, it is in our *being*, which is – at its core, a presence and mindfulness practice – that we find the greatest peace. When we strip away our emotional defenses, our professional accomplishments and even our limited personalities, it leaves us with the quiet space where our awareness, or consciousness, is seated.

I never developed the latter.

I didn't understand how to handle that potent yet quiet space. So I filled it with men, drinking, drugs and everything that didn't belong within me just to fill that void that I could not fill myself. I believe, regardless of where you come from, how old you are or what you look like, we all share that space within. And we all have the opportunity to carve out something new that aligns in more healthy ways.

By 2005, I was playing with 6-figure placements and working for a premier executive search firm in Southern California. I was an Executive recruiter headhunting finance and accounting professionals. I broke 6-figures myself, bought a white picket fence home, got married, but deep inside – I was so miserable.

I had my first relapse at Christmas time in 2007 at a lovely company party. I had not had a drink since 2002. I was convinced that I wasn't an alcoholic and that I could handle my alcohol. This run lasted for over two years and the emotional unmanageability was sheer chaos. I was so determined to prove to myself that I was working the recovery program since I wasn't taking a pill or snorting any white substance up my nose like during my college years. I remember I was so unhappy with all my personal problems at home. This is typical behavior of an alcoholic. Since alcohol was legal and my fun colleagues would party like *Rockstars* at company parties, I felt like I was normal and could too.

We were working professionals by day and party animals by night.

The party didn't last long once I made the decision to sober up again. Work was going great and money was overflowing my bank account. The white picket fence house I bought in Irvine was just perfect. I was mentally prepared to bring a child into the world by the end of 2008. Things were looking up. The biggest problem on my hands was the abusive relationship I had at home with a bipolar manic depressive. At this point, he had already been in and out of several mental wards, emergency rooms during manic episodes and even jail once. We had already been to family court at least a dozen times with several restraining orders. I'm a survivor and have a strong belief that we can push forward through anything. Although I was still in the relationship, I was very skeptical. There were a lot of sleepless nights. Medical binders with medical reports were piling up, but I had contingency plans in place. I was never scared.

By December, 2008, I was a mother. I arranged my life back in order, got financially stable and ferociously began to journal, working the steps in recovery again.

As a sober individual, *life still happens to you* and it will continue to present all its pain, traumas, roller coasters, manic episodes and suffering. I only found Moments of clarity and happiness far and few in between the internal struggles. I forced myself to face the agony from being addicted to alcohol, mind-altering substances and emotional dependencies with men and relationships. For the next few years, I only had intermittent levels of confidence and self-esteem.

I continued to fight more difficult battles that seemed endless.

I hit my second rock bottom. Emotional bottoms were the worst. Although I felt I was on the right path, there were still a lot of things that were not right within my mind, body and spirit. I was still holding onto a lot of childhood traumas, resentments and *character defects that I didn't even realize existed.*

At one point, I checked myself into rehab for two weeks. During that time, I had not fully surrendered so I left the rehab without doing any of the work. It took me a long time to detoxify from the effects of alcoholism. It took me longer to finally learn how to take responsibility for my behaviors. I also recognized that I had been sick for a long time and could not get well without help. I learned addiction would be a lifelong condition but not a permanent impairment. In treatment and therapy, I began to address shame, honesty, self-abuse, self-harm, self-destructiveness and self-abandonment. I attended support groups, met with sponsors, mentors and coaches, and in doing so, my life changed. Many people in my life provided me the inspiration and support I needed as well.

For years, I considered myself a sober woman since I was not popping pills or drinking any longer. I wrote off all my problems as being a part of just growing up. However, it was harder to realize that I was still not *"emotionally sober"* because I was still acting out.

Emotional sobriety is a bitch.

It's so hard to obtain. There were so many things triggering me that caused emotional relapses. I had to get really honest with myself and dig deeper within to truly understand what was going on in other areas of my life to fully heal.

One day it suddenly hit me like a revelation. I was still acting out old addictive emotional patterns of behaviors such as:

- *Internet stalking old and new flings*
- *Controlling others and jealousy fits*
- *Engaging in the codependency dance*
- *Emotional outburst, manipulation*
- *Emotional anorexia, unavailability and euphoria*
- *Excessive sex and addictive love patterns*
- *Stuffing my feelings with food*
- *Comparing myself to others*
- *Playing mind games, guilt trips*
- *Mindlessly bantering and intriguing without intent of relationships*

These were a few behaviors that kept me emotionally charged, in other words "*High.*" I would turn these addictive behaviors towards relationships or other unhealthy behaviors when I was lonely, upset or feeling insecure. My self-worth and self-esteem were tied to having someone to fix and rescue me.

This led me to only attracting toxic relationships once again, because that was the vibration I was sending out and the dynamic I was asking for by embodying it. It was the message I was casting out into the Universe of what I deserve – until I realized I no longer deserved it. Until these toxic patterns and behaviors brought me to my knees, praying and begging to God, the Universe and Source energy – whoever is out there watching out over me – for desperate help.

At this point, I still had many forms of addictive compulsions and chaos, such as reckless sex, love, food, clutter and spending. I found and began discovering other 12 step programs such as SLAA, CODA, DA, CLA, OA, AL-ANON, NA, and PA.

- *AA (Alcoholics Anonymous)*
- *SLAA (Sex & Love Addicts Anonymous)*
- *DA (Debtors Anonymous)*
- *CLA (Clutterers Anonymous)*
- *OA (Overeaters Anonymous)*
- *Al-Anon (Support group for friends/family of the alcoholic)*
- *NA (Narcotics Anonymous)*
- *PA (Pills Anonymous)*

Essentially, there are 12 step recovery programs for just about any type of problem (In fact, there are 254 types of support groups available all around the world!). It is truly up to you to seek the support that is already out there. The beauty of attending these different meetings and listening to the literature, readings and shares, is that each program offers new language and vocabulary to identify, express and work through to the root of our deeper wounds and problems. Naming has potent power to reclaim, to understand and to heal. When we understand something, it is no longer an unknown excuse or foreign threat.

It becomes a part of us that we must integrate and face.

I finally quieted down my mind so that I could hear my heart's desires.

The discovery and commitment to these programs started to make me feel sane again. I was finally healthy, drug-free and thinking clearly. I accepted that my life suddenly took on a new direction. I was open to the changes that this might bring, and I finally *slowed the pace of my life down.*

What kept me coming back to the recovery rooms was the raw honesty and vulnerability. The power of being fully present, fully authentic and fully seen has a healing force beyond measure. I learned how to live life on life's terms. To allow life to *flow with more ease and not resist it.* The most important aspects of my recovery were that it repaired my family relationships, it helped me heal from the sexual trauma and abuse from the past and built uplifting friendships that will last a lifetime. I've seen recovered men and women explore healthy romances, have fulfilling careers and manifest dreams that came with recovery – and that gave me hope.

My story is one of trials, hope, support, recovery and success. I share intimate stories so that you can hear about the human side of addictive disease, its false grip, as well as the confidence and freedom I have gained emerging from this terrifying illness. At last, I allowed God to heal parts of my life that I wasn't able to do on my own.

Surrendering was the key to opening myself to inner growth, inner intimacy, as well as a place of self-love.

The discipline of surrendering and the virtue of humility is necessary for spiritual healing. Other virtues are honesty, acceptance, willingness and open-mindedness. The first step in recovery is to admit complete defeat as stated in Step 1 of the program of AA, which is *"We are powerless over X and our lives have become unmanageable." Listed on pages 59-60 in the Big book of Alcoholics Anonymous.* The admission of powerlessness is the way to recovery. There is hope for those who wish to recover.

Through deep self-reflection and work in the various recovery programs, I was able to truly forgive myself. I believed at one point in my life that I was so unworthy of love and acceptance that I didn't deserve goodness or success. I hid my talents for fear of what it could bring. That was, until one of many Moments where I faced a difficult decision.

Do I move forward, or do I remain as I am right now? Do I keep allowing myself to grow or do I remain stagnant and stuck?

PART TWO

UNWRAPPING YOUR POTENTIAL

CHAPTER FOUR

JOINING THE TWO CATHY'S: HEALING FROM MY PAST INTO MY FUTURE

"You must be the change you wish to see in the world."
—Mahatma Gandhi

Yes, I'm all grown-up now! I'm finally happy and healthy and that's all I've ever wanted in life, but I got even more from this journey than I ever imagined. It finally all came together for me – it all clicked. I have had a lightbulb Moment of awakening. My heart has made it a mission to tell everyone that anything and everything is possible. You name it, I've probably tried it, or it will at least have made it on my bucket list.

Today, I'm able to consciously choose a meaningful lifestyle of *slowing down* to reduce my anxiety level by using the self-Havening practice, as well as through integrating the coaching processes learned throughout the years. I also practice the principles of the 12 step program in all aspects of my life. I made it a commitment to myself and others only to focus on the positive aspects of life and to stick with the "*Program*" as a lifestyle-choice even though I was intermittently in and out of the *"Program"*.

A significant discovery and realization for me is that all of the recovery programs I've taken told me to take *"action."* Not one single program advises us to sit still, *slow down* and just be present. Pressure to take massive action has always been ingrained in me. I created new possibilities every chance I got. I was addicted to external growth. I kept speeding up! Recovery programs are there to help us shift behaviors and give us a new perspective in the world and behave in a certain way that supports our lives. It is a program for living. Yet, I still made contrary, decisive actions and held onto my old belief systems and past experiences, even when it was the hard route of resistance. Now, I am finally creating new shifts in my life to change the direction of its course, no matter how big or small.

There is always something magical that happens as soon as you invest in learning, apply a principle, put pen to paper, work with a coach/sponsor, set intentions of a vision and work towards a future goal on the calendar. You will find that your attitude starts to adjust, becomes optimistic and hopeful. You become excited about what's about to come. Through that, you have the power to change your thought processes and trajectory of life. Like the wise Tony Robbins explains, *"Anything in motion tends to stay in motion."*

I still catch myself trying to seek unhealthy attachments – I've spent so long in my life trying to *STICK* to someone else, as much as I wanted my mother or father, or any love interest to stick to me. Yet, I don't feel like I've attached myself to anyone long enough in a healthy lasting dynamic to fully explore each other honestly and deeply. It might come across as aloof when I keep my emotions guarded, but deep down, there are so many more layers to me and I know to others that I am yearning to explore and understand. First, it starts with me fully understanding and being in touch with my own layers and emotions. This is the internal self-work that leads to everything else aligning externally in relationships.

I'm a strong and independent woman. I always have been, but now I finally recognize the importance of *WHO* I am and *WHAT* I offer. Despite our challenged relationship, my mother still gave me the strength and wisdom to live life as a strong independent woman. I told her about the rape in 2018 –decades after it happened. She hugged me for what was the first time that I could remember – and as we cried, she said that hug was for when I was 15. She loves me more than I could ever know. At that Moment, I wanted to go back in time and tell her two decades ago. I wanted to trust her with the information then. I wanted to forgive her so that I could have forgiven myself.

My life perhaps may have turned out differently if I hadn't buried that secret for as long as I did. That is my wish, but I don't have that power – as much as I'd like, no one can turn back the hands of time. We can only move forward with the wisdom we have gained from the lessons and the pain.

My mother and I finally bonded at that point – and as strong as she is, I could see it in her eyes that it pained her to know her eldest daughter went through that experience. She shared that her younger sister, who has passed away from ovarian cancer, was also a victim of sexual assault during their time in the refugee camp. Finally, at that point, my mother felt and understood all the signs of the brokenness, anxiety and depression that I had been through and why I behaved the way I did.

If only I had told her earlier so she understood sooner.

It is a relief to know that this day finally came and that my mother-daughter connection is healing.

Through my childhood wounds, I had to learn to re-parent myself – to understand both my journey and who I am at a fundamental level and to truly love myself through it. The stories about my past used to be fragmented – no one knew the full paragraph, everyone had a few sentences or words and often it was hard for me to keep it all straight myself. Piecing the paragraphs and stories back together into a full and complete narrative authentic to my voice and heart has been liberating and healing.

I am reclaiming all of the broken pieces back for my own self in this book.

OWNING YOUR STORY

"Blessed is the influence of one true, loving human soul to another." —**George Elliot**

I've owned my story—the good and the terrible, the absolute joys and the embarrassments. Owning your account of your life is the very first step to recognizing that you are a person of worth and someone that matters. You are someone with a past, but you also have a present and a future. You can be someone who loves themselves enough to acknowledge and give value to your own journey. Wayne Dyer, a self-help guru and inspirational leader, who has since passed, once said, "***Don't die with your music still in you.***" Music can be anything, but for me, it's developed into writing. Each note is a word and the crescendos of melody are my exclamation points!

We all have a symphony in us waiting and we must be brave to speak it out into the world for our music to be heard and appreciated. The truth is – writing has changed my life. From journaling daily with deep reflective writing, to writing for work and now putting all of my pieces into one complete book – it has helped me find my calling and provided an opportunity to make an impact on the world. It helped me make a living for my family and take care of myself while giving back to others – paying it forward, always.

"SLOW"-BRIETY

"A teacher affects eternity."
—Henry Adams

It took me a long time to realize that sobriety was not only being sober from drugs and alcohol, it's a new way of life. It is a new way of living. Similar to the word "diet" as it comes from the Greek word "*dieta*" meaning a "*way of life.*" Remember, your diet isn't a means to an end; it's just a level of awareness of how you exist in relation to your food. In the same way, sobriety offers you a new level of consciousness in the way you are living in relation to what you consume and allow into your body and being, whether substance or energy.

It's about becoming a new you. A *YOU* that you can honestly face in the light of day with pride and love. Living life slowly, cherishing every experience and fully being present in every minute as if it's the best Moment of your life are the gifts you will receive. Today, I can't imagine facing life in any other way. I share my story so that you know you, too, can embark successfully upon this transformative soul journey. There will be a lot of painful Moments, heartbreaks and tears along the way. Change is a series of small committed steps that add up to a great outcome. It may take a long time and be discouraging at times, but I promise you it will be worth it. You will be able to look in the mirror, see the version of your best self, full of integrity, love and life.

WHAT IS ACCEPTANCE?

"Acceptance to me feels like learning how to live in slow motion and falling into an undercurrent that sweeps me gently and peacefully away. Each slow deep breath draws me closer to the person I am supposed to be."
—Cathy Trinh, Journal entry – *January 01, 2020*

Acceptance allows you to be a healthy, confident, self-loving and free person. It's quite beautiful and poetic as we surrender to being in the present. Acceptance is trust in allowing the Universe to help orchestrate a grander plan and flow of life. Acceptance, by its very nature, is imperfect, often unpleasant – while ultimately leading to a place of growth, a sense of freedom and a life of ease. I know this because I had to painfully accept so many areas of my life, to help me get fear and suffering unstuck within myself. Through complete self-acceptance and true acceptance of life itself, I opened myself to the beauty of Moments of synchronicities and signs that guide the way. When I truly listened, was in acceptance, surrendered to my divine path and greater flow, I received so much more cosmic blessings than when I was in painful resistance. Pain is resistance. Acceptance ultimately paves the way to a spiritual freedom knowing all is happening for the greatest good and in perfect divine timing.

Years ago, I was in the unnatural state of striving for achievement, fun-seeking, and often reckless ways of living. I ignored clues my body was giving me to alert me of danger. I pushed and hid what my body was feeling and it came to a screeching halt with my cancer diagnosis in 2018. After being diagnosed with thyroid cancer that had spread to eight of my lymph nodes, attached to my carotid artery and vocal nerve, I gave up an active social life and the self-image that had propped me up in the world for all those years. This significant life event forced me to go within to seek inner strength and healing.

I started taking meditation classes and applied Buddhist practices to my daily life: sitting silently, feeling my body breathing, listening to hear what was within and around me. I accepted that there was no going back, that this diagnosis was only the beginning of a door opening to where life might lead me. *Slowly living* life feels like trusting that the earth will support all of my weight, all my heaviness, all of my physical pain and mental anguish. It is trusting that it will bring me to a place of feeling grounded, a place that's ready to respond with wisdom and compassion. By doing this, you too, will let go of the past, feel free, experience happiness and create a fulfilling future.

From that point forward, I made a personal decision to live a sober life for good. I chose to take back control of my life from the abuse of emotional and destructive behaviors. Abstaining from what I identified and named as "*baseline behaviors*" is the only way to live to free myself from the chains of addiction and old toxic patterns. The only way for me is to completely abstain from it.

Having the opportunity to learn how to live a good and peaceful life was extraordinary. In recovery, I received unconditional love and acceptance. The gradual process of recovery helped mend my broken heart and pulled me back from depths of despair. I met a lot of amazing friends on my journey. When you're battling an addiction, (remember it comes in many forms), take the time to seek out treatment not just for your addiction, but for your soul – your spiritual well-being.

That comes in many forms, too!

FACING SEX & LOVE ADDICTION

"There are two ways of meeting difficulties: You alter the difficulties or you alter yourself to meet them."
—Phyllis Bottome

My addiction to relationships was one of the hardest problems to overcome. After years of destructive and volatile relationships, one after another, I finally realized I was getting high off relationships. This honest realization blew my mind. I came to understand that my self-worth and self-esteem had been tied to the constant need for validation from people and especially men, to prove my worth. I was boy crazy and had chased them like I chased my drugs, alcohol and food. And the results were often thoughtless and self-harming.

Being Vietnamese-American growing up during a time of great confusion in America, I have made a lot of poor choices on my dating journey. I have dated the absolutely ugh-worthy, impulsive slackers, confused players, obsessive, co-dependent, sex-crazed weirdos. I have also dated heart-wrenching Romeos. I've dated cheaters; I have also been the cheater. I have engaged in guilt-tripping and shame ridden relationships that took me forever to walk away from. I have dealt with long-lost creepers that wouldn't leave me alone. I, too, was a creeper, so I can relate to that mindset!

Confusion coupled with not having guidance was a big aspect of my failed relationships. Being the eldest of three girls in my family with parents busy working, and being an executive recruiter by trade, my adventure of finding and dating men were like cattle calls. I used the shotgun approach style, usually an effective strategy in recruiting when you first start off as a rookie recruiter to herd prospective candidates in by the dozens. This approach really never yielded any promising life-long partners, and it had dragged more brokenness into my life. Maybe it was because of my Asian upbringing, lessons I wasn't taught or being the eldest with no real role model, I was not adequately trained. *Whatever it was, it sure was painful!* Dating was a joke. Online dating was a nightmare. And social media and growing up in the age of the internet killed all of my relationships---*even the ones I wasn't really even in!*

During my online dating escapades, I unintentionally and literally turned into the world's biggest online stalker. It was so humiliating; no grace and no dignity whatsoever! Being a recruiter doesn't help. I am always researching and have to be *"in the know"*. I even made a long rap sheet on an Excel spreadsheet (the "Black Book") where I catalogued names, dates and characteristics of men I've dated with pros and cons as a way of tracking my progress in relationships. Among the rap sheet ranged from the emotional unavailable, obsessive compulsive, alpha-male narcissist, to deranged psychopaths, business executives to the unemployed. I always felt like I was several steps ahead of the men I dated through methodical research and manipulative ways. I knew when they woke up. I timed delayed my responses to make it appear I am not too eager. I pretended not to care when I was really fuming because they gave their Instagram or Facebook more attention than me. I projected what I was going to say in a conversation that wasn't even happening at the moment--- conversations that were happening only in my own head! And when I suspected them of being dishonest, I created fake social media accounts to catch them in the act. I was constantly chasing and seeking justice and subjected my emotions through a sea of storms. I was basically a man's worst nightmare, but the reality is that I felt powerless inside. Stalking men on the internet is so shameful but it kept me high and wanting more.

At one point I came to realize that what I was trying to do is find love in someone who would love me the way I thought love was, which is to feel cared for and wanted. Through the program, as I turned inward, I learned how to love myself and trust myself before I can seek it from outside.

With men, I have been through the extreme of highs and lows. I wasn't able to live with them, but I also wasn't able to live without them. Sometimes I went on endless dates with cringe-worthy guys and couldn't help but question my sanity. I saw a funny meme that read, *"If you line up all your ex-lovers in a row you can see a flow chart of your mental illness.* That was me in a nutshell.

Looking back now, I cringe because as I was searching for my identity I broke a lot of hearts, left relationships hanging, hurt people, but worse of all broke my own heart along the way. They say that *"hurt people, hurt people."* As I took inventory of my Sex & Love addiction during the cleansing and detox period, I am able to see my character defects that I have shown during all my relationships. I saw that I was in a constant need of approval, of people pleasing, of preserving my self-image. I saw that I did not have clear boundaries with men. All this led to me feelings of self-pity, feelings of being unlovable, feelings of being unattractive, unworthy, and inadequate.

There were so many horror stories, some were so upsetting, embarrassing and generally so terrible I couldn't tell anyone about. One time I dated a man I met on a dating app. After having ten drinks at a red carpet charity event in Beverly Hills, I ended up puking in his new Maserati. The Maserati he just pulled out of the dealership that same day! I called this story the *"Maserati story,"* because I ended up the following day in a Beverly Hills hotel hungover and alone with his Maserati bag with him nowhere to be found. I kept that poor bag months later until I decided to discard it down a trash shoot. While some women are given diamonds and fancy things, my trophy was his bag with my vomit still inside after a marathon of drinking one night. Good thing he didn't want the bag back and we lost touch, because I discovered he and his three friends were under investigation by the FBI after months of surveillance for a concert scam. Thanks dating app for the short romance and lead, whose name I will choose to remain anonymous!

Another time I met a man a few months after I made my way back into the S.L.A.A. program. In early recovery, it is usually advised we stay away from relationships during the first year of sobriety. This way we can detoxify our minds, bodies and spirit. As our friendship developed, I started spotting signs and unhealthy patterns of behaviors I recognized in myself while I was in active addiction. I recognize in him the urges, the impulses, the desires of being loved and wanted. He called me ten to fifteen times throughout the day with the need for support, and became angry and demeaning when he couldn't get his way. It was so consuming that it took me away from taking care of myself and fulfilling my parental responsibilities. And when I was not there for him, I felt guilty for not being a good friend. But I needed to set boundaries, so I chose to protect my own well-being and let him go. My biggest concern was when he stopped showing up to support group meetings, which was a sign of not taking his recovery seriously.

After eight months of disconnect from this man, I learned that he was found dead in a car from a drug overdose. The news of his death shocked and saddened me because I prayed for him with the hopes he would get the help he needed. My wish was for him to get better and to have a chance of living a normal happy life after a lifetime battling addition, but this was no longer available for him. I've made peace with this and other relationships on my journey. I have promised to myself to continually work the program and make living amends for the missteps from past relationships by treating everyone on my new path with respect and dignity from now on.

I have shared a few of these stories to shed light on my messy and imperfect life. I had so many shameful relationship flaws and ways I related to coping with people. I was an open book who overshared and inevitably *"trauma-bonded"* with everyone. I thought this was an effective way of communicating and building connections. However, I recognized later I was only playing the victim, martyr and manipulated my way into relationships with emotional attachments. As far as I can remember, I was always enmeshed or entangled in one relationship or another. After leaving one relationship, I would show up at another person's door with a big trash bag of emotional wreckage, debris and remnants from the past or recent turmoil. Sadly, sometimes with one or more emotional liaisons at a time, desperately seeking that feeling of validation I could not find from one source. This was because I was unfulfilled within my own self.

My recruiting career allowed me to interact with all kinds of people. Receiving approval from clients helped solidify me and keep my pride as well as ego intact. My sparkly personality became a detriment at times because I attracted all kinds of people into my life – sometimes not positive ones.

As an overachiever, my love life turned into a big game and the hunt became more competitive as time went on. A harsh reality I faced was that I was attracted to emotionally dangerous situations. I attracted brokenness and trauma into my life. One of my default ways to relate to others was to "rescue" and "fix" everyone, only to find myself wandering aimlessly and mindlessly through life caught up with toxic people who kept me high and distracted, not allowing space in my life to grow or take care of myself. This problem unveiled a bitter and honest look at my behavior and I caught onto the idea that it was a disease of the mind, a form of mental illness for me.

I wanted more and I wanted it faster. Slow living with intentional mindfulness was extremely lacking in my life.

The recovery program I was in helped me get centered and learn to have a relationship with myself first. Gradually, relationships with others took on a stronger foundation. Working the steps helped peel back the layers of the onion, making the harsh fact come to light that I was raised in a dysfunctional, emotionally anorexic and verbally abusive Asian household. We all had a hard time expressing ourselves. I felt betrayed, violated and emotionally unbalanced with the sheer chaos at home and it poured into all my adult relationships. Our childhood wounds inform our adult broken patterns and decisions if we have not done the healing work to address them at the root cause and source of origin. I was very comfortable being in psychological warfare and there was hardly ever any peace in my house. Home life was not emotionally safe to turn to and it spiraled into years of untrustworthy romantic relationships I attracted but eventually ran from. I returned to destructive relationships because it was comfortable and familiar. My emotional and nervous systems get adjusted to a certain level of stress stimulants as a child and I continued the pattern into adulthood because it's what my body and mind were used to.

I lost track of how many times I would block a phone number, delete online dating apps, vowing to stop online stalking but finding myself unblocking, uploading and snooping again in a few days. Funny enough, I once lost a $1,000 bet to a friend who tried to help me stay away from a toxic ex-lover.

I married young. This marriage was a very enmeshed and codependent relationship that wreaked havoc in my life, but it was also a relationship that saved my life from drug addiction and gave me the most beautiful gift in the form of my son.

"God has orchestrated scenarios to test me all my life, just as the Universe puts you through many difficult lessons on your path to help you learn and grow. There is no way out of learning from the teacher of Life."
—**Journal entry,** *June 21, 2019*

One time, the Universe orchestrated an ex-boyfriend to move into an apartment right below me in a complex with over 500 units. He lived below me for one whole lease cycle. The Universe perhaps sent me a symbolic message that physically I had dated down, I had lowered my values, morals and standards by being involved with that person who brought further trauma and chaos into my life. It was not a coincidence that he moved in right below me. There are no coincidences in life. I spent months running away from this person and there he was, only several feet of distance below me. There was no more running away from facing the emotions this broken relationship brought up within me and how I allowed myself to be further wounded by it.

Our relationship lasted for over three years. We originally met at another apartment complex. Instantly, we became lovers. I took no time to get to know him. Yet another stranger that I befriended and emotionally bonded to and moved quickly. Another person I did not take the time to get to know. I noticed some red flags but chose to ignore the visible signs.

For months with him living below me, it was so hard. It was very emotionally difficult because love was still present. Not everything in that relationship was bad. I met him a few years ago during a time that I was trying to heal. I stayed with him and gave the relationship a chance hoping I could be in a healthy, normal and lasting relationship finally. But it was far from healing. This ex-lover brought more chaos, distrust, lies and low self-esteem into my life. One time, at a paint event I helped a friend organize, he showed up drunk and got more and more obnoxious as the evening went on arguing with me incessantly. When asked to leave, it broke out into a fight and he violently threw a chair across the floor at the guests. He had to be physically removed by my friend's husband while kicking and screaming, all the while threatening to fight. I tried to restrain and stop him. I broke down and cried in deep humiliation in front of all of the guests and my friends. My friends comforted me and advised me to break it off with that boyfriend. That event was a pivotal Moment that made me realize this relationship was more toxic than it was rewarding.

Yet, I still continued in that relationship, becoming the enabler. Shortly after, I found he was secretly talking to multiple women who were apparently "*old friends*" and also illegally sending private photos of me taken without my knowledge, as a card trading game on a text chain with several other male friends. This brought on great distrust and shame, as well as low self-esteem. I was with a partner who was cheating and seeking attention elsewhere without honest communication. *I finally broke free from this relationship when I realized I needed to focus on my own healing* and my son. In retrospect, this broken dynamic taught me about my self-worth and what I do deserve, symbolic of when he moved downstairs and I was forced to revisit these lessons and emotions, but with a clearer perspective.

The heart wrenching relationship between this man and me was extremely toxic, but it had to happen and the experience needed to be gained. It was one of the most exciting but also the worst I ever encountered. I had always characterized our union as being the wildest ride I had to be on to find my true self. He was charming, loving and care-free, similar to me. However, he also had his flaws and secrets. We locked ourselves in a painful drama-filled relationship where neither of us felt satisfied or sufficiently loved. It was painful for both of us, as we always blamed each other for the pain we created for one another. With this man, I had a miscarriage where I bled out alone on my bed and then a second pregnancy where I chose to abort without his involvement. One day I was all in and then the next day, I ran away. I had mistreated others, just like he mistreated me; I never felt like we were both ever enough for each other. I am sure I carried the pain and hurt from my past relationships, always processing, searching and working on healing what's broken inside of me, but not knowing how to successfully heal me.

People come into our lives for a reason, season or lesson. Without a questionable shadow of a doubt, I know today that this man was the mirror into the depths of the darkness within me. He allowed me to see all my character defects and the games I had been playing with other people. The hurt I had caused. The amends that had to be made. Only until I was able to see and recognize these traits could I move into living a thoughtful existence and beautiful life. Looking back today, I was extremely active in my sex and love addiction when I was involved with him. I was desperate for love, attention and validation. The intense drama helped me numb my pain from my painfully abusive marriage.

Returning to painful and destructive relationships was a pattern that had repeated over and over for me – punishing one another, not trusting one another and depriving one another of free expression. During other Moments, I was infatuated and sought attention from the wrong people.

I couldn't handle the love that I was being showered with from nice men, always waiting for the shoe to drop until they left me and the only answer was to leave those relationships first. With this particularly toxic relationship, I knew the only way to get well was complete abstinence and I finally left the relationship for good.

Throughout my life, I was like an enslaved warrior who hunted and broke the hearts of many men. Despite any love that I was showered with, I couldn't trust anyone with my heart. For so long, I remained aloof and arrogant in relationships. Not to mention the multiple careless pregnancies from unprotected affairs and then the consequences of abortions. All led me to where I am today and painfully learn what I do understand now.

Since I was seventeen, I was very sexually active and careless with unprotected sex and intense love addiction. I have been pregnant six times throughout my life – with four abortions, one miscarriage and one healthy wanted son. I have never used protection to avoid accidental pregnancies and sexually contracted diseases with the multiple encounters with men, strangers and non-committed relationships. It was completely reckless, in the same way I approached drug use and alcohol. Luckily, I never caught any diseases that I could have passed along to another lover. There were plenty of lessons learned from this reckless behavior. Only later, I found out that sex, in the highest form, is an expression of deep connection in a nurturing and loving relationship. I never referred to sex as "Making love." I am still working on this new language of love. This was an eye-opening Moment for me. There have been so many opportunities to learn and grow that I didn't realize until later. Had I *slowed down* and truly reflected, I might have made the changes sooner.

When reflecting back on this intoxicating and broken relationship, I often question why I kept coming back.

What lessons did I need in order to learn and grow through? What did I not learn? Why was I still so angry and bitter? What was God trying to tell me?

The magnitude of the situation showed me that I was still sick and it is a progressive disease if I let him back in. I hit my last rock bottom again in all areas of my life and with the help of the program, I went back to complete abstinence. Ultimately, I learned a huge lesson that facing my own shadows and broken self through these relationships served as mirror reflections of my wounds that needed healing.

It took me months of white-knuckling that situation trying to hold on, but inside, I knew I had a significant problem on my hands. I was deeply emotionally attached to this person. The pain was connected to pleasure, like an addiction. The only way to break free from the grips of this addiction was to focus on my own healing, work on me and what I wanted for my own future.

I had to find the person I wanted to become.

I know I was an addict because I had the habit of rushing into relationships without getting to know these men. When I did this, I would also glitch out on problems with money and social media. There were always signs of sex and love addiction. Yet, I chose to ignore them and refused to acknowledge them as destructive, for fear of loneliness and abandonment. The relationships always slowly burned, but I needed to experience them so that I could learn and finally, deeply realize the self-love and self-respect that I deserved in a relationship and how I treated my own self.

Within the years prior, I was entirely in my disease and not working on myself in a program. I was addicted to the emotional intensity and newness that came from people I met. That initial excitement and hope of new love's potential. I was hardly ready for a relationship and was still emotionally, mentally, and spiritually sick when I tried to get into them. I played my own games and got burned by manipulation, lies, withholding of control, and broken love.

I eventually was able to treat myself like a precious object because it made me feel healthy and strong. I began to crave sobriety and dedicate my life to long-term sobriety. I corrected my own behavior through the recovery program and abstained from the rescuer mentality. I used to treat all of my relationships like two ships that passed one another in the night, with no lasting connection or consequences. Today, I'm so much happier and aware of my toxic patterns. I learned what loneliness was. For the first time in my life, I learned how to feel okay being alone. I ended up taking a 12-month vow of sacred devotion and became abstinent and celibate from the following:

- *No dating for one year*
- *No sex and pornography (detoxed from the euphoria of the mind and body high sensations)*
- *No social media (to remove daily distractions and triggers associated with social media)*
- *No posting anything that would get unwanted attention*
- *No internet stalking former lovers on social media platforms*
- *No going to bars and clubs with intentions of intriguing*
- *No one night stands, friends with benefit relationships, no contact with qualifiers, online dating sites, flirting or sending sexually explicit dialogue.*

I consciously decided not to spend time with men, even as friends. Instead, *I put all of my time and energy into building deeper sisterhood relationships with other women.* This was a game changer for me. By healing my feminine energy and connections, I started to see myself changing. I was beginning to transform into the person I knew existed. Someone who was lost a long time ago. I read poetry and listened to my favorite music. I studied self-empowerment videos and familiarized myself with professional social media marketing strategies to improve my business. I focused on my health, wellness, spirituality, my son, re-centered my priorities and grounded myself in ways I haven't during my entire life.

I finally removed all of the distractions and substance abuse that had been part of my life since I was thirteen years old. I finally felt real feelings for the first time in twenty-seven years.

I sat with my cravings for both substances and male comfort or companionship. On some nights, it felt like loneliness, but the happiness, joy, peace endured and the feelings of sadness and failure began to dissipate. During my active addiction, I was unable to feel anything. I couldn't feel real joy. I had forgotten how much I loved music and poetry. For the first time in twenty-seven years, I was completely sober. I finally felt deep joy and appreciation in it!

Back then, if I wasn't involved in one relationship after another, I was looking for the next best weight loss fad to feel better about myself. The only thing I was inhaling was cigarettes and realized it was an unhealthy way for me to cope as well, so I had to also get rid of that habit. I became vice-less. I also was not able to use food as a way to cope because I was on a strict diet through all of my cancer treatments. Thus, I was left with my own raw self.

I was face to face with me. Just me.

I then found humor, awareness and peace in the rooms of AA and SLAA again. I loved going to meetings because other people could relate, had similar struggles and passed no judgment in my shares of my problems and adventures. I finally enjoyed my life even though it was mainly working, the recovery program, lots of journaling and introspection. When people ask me what love addiction is, or how to overcome it, I answer that it's the same way you overcome any other obsession, slowly but committedly. *Love addiction had been playing out in my life, long before I ever became addicted to substances.* Learning how to be alone, cleaning up my life and decluttering in all aspects of my life was vital to overcoming my love addiction.

I withdrew from social media and social texting chain interactions to help quiet down my life, my language and control any negativity from entering my life as it slipped through the cracks of unwanted text replies. Cutting back on social media was the best thing I did, as I became aware that it had gotten completely out of control, affecting my self-image and self-esteem. I discovered a gentle and loving way to speak to myself and others. It was eye-opening for me because I realized it was the way I wanted to speak to myself – to that inner child that needed gentleness, compassion and love. I wanted to become a better influence on my friends and set a good example for my son.

It had to first start with me.

I have learned so much about myself through my journey of recovery. Today, I respect my body more than I ever have before. I have developed a deep and meaningful relationship with my God, Higher Power and I have trust in the Universe. I am fully aware that I am no longer alone with my efforts to heal myself from an addiction of any sort. My vulnerability allows me to have the capacity to trust, which has been restored by my deepened faith in the process.

My whole life strategy of the chase of sexual intrigue, romantic connections and emotional dependency had to be surrendered in order for me to heal.

Healing meant I let go of all of these old toxic patterns.

Eventually, I learned to abandon situations that put me at risk physically, spiritually, psychologically and morally in order for me to grow. I learned how to accept and love myself, take care of responsibility for my own life and my individual needs, before I associated myself with others. I was able to ask for help, allow myself to be vulnerable, learn to trust and accept others in my life. I allowed myself to work through the anguish of low self-esteem, fears of abandonment and fears of failure. I eventually felt comfortable in solitude and felt at peace for the first time in my life. I began to accept all of my imperfections and past mistakes as a part of being human. I began to heal from shame, remorse, self-abandonment, distrust, pride, ego, avoidance, excessiveness, vanity, gluttony, self-image issues… the list of character traits I let go goes on and on.

In recovery, I finally have victory over the past. I substituted honesty and integrity for self-destructive and self-seeking ways of expressing emotions. I became authentic, was able to truly express who I am and developed real intimacy within myself and others. Finally, I was able to restore back to healthier ways of being and living on a daily basis. The obsessive behavior has left me and my relationships with men and women are more healthy and trusting. I now have a number of long-term successful friendships with men as I've worked on and learned how to love myself first. I'm proud to say I now have life-long healthy relationships with men in my circle that include business men within my peer group, men whom I trust to offer me healthy advice on life, agenda-free men whom I trust to reach out to when I'm having a hard day, and men who truly love and respect me for the person I am. I'm so grateful and blessed to reach this point of unconditional love in my life.

I had to fully engage in my recovery as a priority.

CHAPTER FIVE

MENTORS/COACHES/SPONSORS/GURUS

"I am not a teacher, but an awakener."—**Robert Frost**

Before really working any recovery program, I had a habit of running away from relationships, family, friends, mentors, coaches and sponsors. I intentionally ran away from facing the cold hard truth of my brokenness. Close relationships are our mirrors into our own selves. I struggled with intimacy. For years, I struggled to find the right person to partner with, especially in the areas of recovery, coaching and mentorship. I moved fast into relationships, was a very needy person and I would cling to the first person I felt could save me. Now, I've learned to take my time to get to know someone before committing to a relationship with them. This process had to start with me. I had to trust and love myself enough to allow myself to trust others.

The rules finally changed.

I stopped dancing the codependent waltz.

This same rule now applies to every romantic relationship or partnership I get into in life. Whether in recovery program, business, or love, boundaries were set. I approach them now with thoughtful intentions and honesty. Finding the right sponsor, coach or mentor is so important. It is very important that you find a mentor or sponsor based on your needs and how you work together. Some sponsors set firm boundaries with their availability and phone times, while others are more available and flexible with when you can reach out to them. Some sponsors and coaches are in the right place in their lives and will take the time to learn about you. A good sponsor, coach or mentor will make sure their experience level and personality are aligned with your needs. Those who also know how to communicate in these areas are the most effective and best person to work with. Everything hinges on communication.

Every day, I remind myself that I am truly a powerful force of love and freedom, here to inspire greatness in myself and others. I get to enjoy and have fun and embrace the ability to create the life I love. I am so blessed to have the roles of mother, teacher, protector, nurturer and guide for my son to help him learn how to fulfill his own needs the best ways he can on his own journey.

I have grown exponentially on my journey. Being single and not searching for others to fulfill my life has allowed me to discover who I truly am.

I am on a path of profound self-discovery so that when I'm ready to be in a healthy relationship, I will have the right mindset to be in that relationship.

I'm excited to be on this journey of self-recovery. I use the gifts of the programs to create new possibilities for me and my life. Being free from substance and emotional abuse has given me clarity and clearer vision of how to move into the future. I have learned so much on my journey. I am whole and complete today, whereas before I was incomplete with others and myself. I no longer "*Trauma Bond*" anymore. This is a concept termed by Patrick Carnes. Trauma bonding is when you bond with someone because of their traumas.

"It occurs as the result of ongoing cycles of abuse in which the intermittent reinforcement of reward and punishment creates powerful emotional bonds that are resistant to changes." "It is the misuse of fear, excitement, sexual feelings and sexual physiology to entangle with another person based on shared traumas,"
—**Patrick Carnes, PhD.** Betrayal Bond: Breaking Free from Exploitive Relationships.

Being the primary aggressor in this game, I leaned toward extreme, risk-taking behaviors and this type of bonding was a huge factor in all my relationships. I had beat relationships to a pulp. I was mean, spiteful, vile and had narcissistic tendencies. Even the half-decent partnerships would go from fun to Moments of sheer chaos, disappointment and utterly toxicity in a matter of months. I was not a stranger at the courthouse obtaining restraining orders, playing the blocking and unblocking game with men's phone numbers and social media profiles because I couldn't stay away and was addicted to the drama. Some relationships took years and others took only months to hit rock bottom with my toxic behavior. I know I masked my problems with my need to feel loved and validated.

To take a closer look at how the program of S.L.A.A. (Sex & Love Addicts Anonymous) works, it is essential to know that the addiction is a disease. It is a disease of the mind. Everything starts within your mind. This program helped me relearn and reframe healthy boundaries. As addicts, we have never had any boundaries, let alone clear boundaries for ourselves. Through working the steps, I figured out my emotionally toxic and dangerous accessory behaviors. I *"cleaned house"* and was more mindful of what I was putting out into the world. I changed how I dressed or interacted with others by text. In order to stay emotionally sober, I avoided all outbursts of anger or rage via text messaging. I could not have any emotional relapses. Sobriety in this program was hard, as it is not as black and white as it is in the alcohol or drug program. There are so many grey areas. Crossing over grey areas and undefined behaviors could cause a relapse.

This is a strict program to follow, but once I hit a certain time in the program milestones – I started to feel a new freedom that I'd never felt before. The withdrawal phase in S.L.A.A. was the worst since the area where love exists in the brain is in the same area as where heroin addicts feel the high. I was the queen of relapse. I'm a social person and crave connectivity, therefore I need to be careful with myself because at any given time I could fall prey to my desires and lust for someone or something that was not healthy for me. For over 15 years, I have to admit I was not able to keep emotionally sober. I ran in and out of meetings with new wreckage, much pain and desperation every couple of years. What kept me coming back was the fellowship and the women in the program.

I finally got serious about working the program and took the steps into healing my life, my heart and my mind. I am living proof that the 12-step-plan laid out in the basic text book of the program works. I am finally living a life beyond my wildest dreams because of it and I am deeply grateful.

SLOWING DOWN IN S.L.A.A.

"Courage is resistance to fear, mastery of fear, not absence of fear." —**Mark Twain**

S.L.A.A. taught me how to love myself and take better care of myself through self-care. This particular 12-step program taught me how to *slow down* some areas of my life – something I never was able to do before. Here are a few things I learned while working the program to help slow down while being in relationships or forming new ones.

- ***Being more thoughtful:*** Slowing down allowed me to develop more thoughtful responses. Being in a technology-driven age, we can interact and move so fast in and out of dialogue with people via phone, text and email. Social media also diminishes the quality of the connection with individuals. Being more thoughtful in your words, actions and connections cultivate deeper bonds within yourself and others.
- ***Know how you feel:*** Slowing down allows you to understand how you feel versus rushing in with racing thoughts and responses throughout the day. Understanding how you feel first helps you form healthier responses that meet your own needs as well as make you more grounded and have greater respect for you and others.
- ***Better relationships:*** Slowing down allows you to be mature, honest and understand yourself. Only then will you lead the life you desire without hurting people around you.
- ***Quality relationships*:** Slowing down allows you to develop more quality relationships of deeper connection.
- ***Create morning routines that support you:*** Slowing down will enable you to create a morning routine that helps your well-being, such as quiet time, mediation, breakfast and journaling. I avoided doing these things when I was distracted by taking care of others, but realized how important they are to my wellness and growth.
- ***Implement Creative Outlets**:* Slowing down allows you to have more time to implement creative outlets and flex creative muscles. It will help keep you engaged and healthily motivated with

others. Moving fast interfered with my ability to perform well and disengaged me from taking care of myself.

- ***Increase a Diet of Positive Emotions:*** Slowing down allows you to feel and choose a diet of positive emotions. Positive emotions build your resilience, creativity and ability to be solution-focused.
- ***Have clear and healthy boundaries:*** Slowing down allows you to focus on what feels right for you and having integrity with yourself and others – allowing you to respect your personal needs and desires.
- ***Slow down your dating pace:*** Slowing down allows you to get to know someone before you get involved with them. Being in my addiction, I dated too quickly before getting to know men and it hurt me and others in the long run with a cycle of addictive behaviors.

Not only did I learn how to slow down, I learned how to tone down my overly sparkly personality while not letting it dull my shine.

I no longer sought comfort or shelter from my brokenness. I took responsibility for my life and owned every outcome each day. I maintained sobriety and emotional wellness by having integrity with my program and everything else in my life.

I treated the program like how one would manage their business - with integrity and respect.

It was vital for me to have integrity with my word and not cut corners to ensure successful outcomes. Most importantly, I had to identify my problems and have the desire to get out of active addiction. I wanted to go deeper into my psyche and understand what was going on.

And I did exactly that.

SLOW DIMENSIONS OF LOVE

"I carry your heart with me (I carry it in my heart)."
—E.E. Cummings

Returning back to the topic of dysfunctional relationships, back in early 2015, I broke off a three month engagement with a man I met on a dating website – where I was seeking a long-term relationship for love and marriage. There were so many red flags in this relationship – questionable social media activity, communication breakdowns and inconsistency in other areas of our relationship. By no means, would I say I was being my best version of me in that relationship. This man was hearing impaired. When our relationship started going downhill I blamed his disability for our communication problems. We were arguing and bickering all the time on text messaging. Perhaps I was in my active addiction, being in fantasy mode, as our reality was more virtual than in-person because of his hearing impairment?

Did I walk away too soon without giving the relationship a chance?

I will never know what would have happened if I remained in that relationship. And I will never know the full truth of what the Universe had in store at the time. *I just knew I wasn't happy.* Looking back now, that relationship needed to happen for me to gain the experience. By the end of the fifth month, after discovering a few inconsistencies from his past, I hopped on a plane and detoured to Paris with girlfriends instead of going on a pre-planned trip to Thailand with this man. Unfortunately, I shut the door to that relationship and never looked back.

Ghosted.

By the end of 2015, I was feeling strong, confident and ready to open the door to dating again. Interestingly enough, the Universe played a weird joke and brought another man into my life with a similar disability. Whether it was destiny or coincidence, this next lover was also hearing impaired. The second hearing impaired man I fell in love with within one year. This lover also had deafness in both ears. I told myself, "*I got this,*" since I just got out of a relationship with one earlier in the year. I thought I was able to handle this relationship and thought it was a sign that this man needed to be in my life for some odd reason.

As my friend and mentor Miss Cathy would always say *"It's not odd, it's God"*. The relationship with the second hearing impaired man lasted for over three years, but it was the most painful relationship I have been in. I learned a lot about myself being in that relationship. I learned that social media was not the problem. It was the person behind the social media that was the problem. There were so many mixed messages that people would send out into the world.

As much as I was trying to use the tools and knowledge I had from the program, my old toxic patterns of behaviors came back and kicked into gear. I was "*white-knuckling the program.*" A dry love addict in active addiction, not working a program. As I was chasing this person around to figure out who he was, I saw levels of my old behaviors that I tried fixing for all these years resurface. It was almost like a game to see how high my pain threshold was. I was so love addicted and codependent for the next three years, which broke me and made me question my sanity. He was broken too and he became the mirror into my past of who I used to be and the games I played. He beat me to my old games and it drove me insane. I was so lost and confused in that relationship. I felt defeated.

Even though there were a lot of breakdowns in this relationship, there was much goodness too. There was a lot of love, tenderness, fun and appreciation, but on the flip side there was also many secrets, codependency, lies and unhealed wounds that we both hadn't worked through on our own. *But the good always comes with the bad.* He made me realize I was not ready to be in a relationship because I hadn't fully learned how to love myself and to have a healthy relationship with myself.

I surrendered and once again returned to the S.L.A.A. program in 2018. I had to work the steps again, go over what happened and why I allowed it to happen.

What made me give up my recovery? Did I start thinking I was cured and I could this work on my own? Where was my relationship with my Higher Power in all of this?

"Without God, no program, honesty and faith, nothing works!"
—**Journal entry**, *January 13th, 2019*

I worked the steps to uncover the toxic patterns that kept showing up again – lack of boundaries with dating toxic men and the constant search for something to fill the God-sized hole in my heart. Whether it was alcohol, shopping, work, overeating or drugs, I used them all to mask emotional addiction in relationships. I had to relearn healthy boundaries again. I fought this problem because I was in denial. I was so desperate to find answers. I continued to look for love in all the wrong places. I was drenched with the *"Gift of Desperation"*. Life was so unmanageable and I was so incomplete, emotionally bankrupt with no peace in my heart. As I was running away from relationships and blaming toxic men for the failed relationships, I made an earth-shattering realization that *I was the unhealthy, toxic person men needed to stay away from in my relationships.*

My addictive, toxic patterns and behaviors of playing games, abuse, jealousy, rage, anger, self-sabotage and victimhood mentality reared its ugly head once again. I wanted perfection from all these "***X's***", but I had unrealistic goals of being perfect myself. I became rigorously honest with myself. I had to learn to let go of my old self and almost all toxic people, places and things.

I fully surrendered and slowed down.

CHAPTER SIX

THANK GOD!

"Lord, make me an instrument of your peace; where there is hatred, let me sow love; where there is injury, pardon; where there is discord, union; where there is doubt, faith; where there is despair, hope; where there is darkness, light; and where there is sadness, joy." —**A prayer of St. Francis of Assisi**

My journey in faith was an interesting one. I grew up as a Buddhist and practiced Buddhism all my life. By age twenty, the Universe had revealed God to me at least a dozen times in the five or more years' prior but I didn't want to listen. I was too afraid of being punished for all the sins and pain I caused myself and others. No one knew how badly I suffered. I saw that God's seed of love had been planted along my journey by other people, the program and friends all this time. Ultimately, I turned my will over to the care of a *Higher Power.*

"I had to relinquish all of my control in order to heal."
—**Journal entry**, *January 30, 2019*

Going through Step four in the program helped me peel the layers of the onion, unpack my story again and heal all parts of my life. Step Four in the 12-step program is *"Make a searching and fearless moral inventory of ourselves."* One of the most important requirements for sobriety is the necessity to recognize and confess our personality defects – a moral inventory – in order to live a life of freedom. You do this by working with a sponsor, counselor, spiritual advisor or coach to make sure you are ready to begin taking this step. Many people get stopped up until this point because the pain of dredging up memories long buried away is too much to look at and endure. Or they use a thousand excuses to not look at their wreckage or part in the problem. The pain of working this step does not come in the writing of the inventory, but it comes from the resistance of looking at where you have been wrong in your life. The mistakes you have made and people you have hurt. Some addicts would rather act out and be loaded than have to face inner truths or as some would call them, *"inner demons."* The freedom from self is made when you let go of fears and secrets you've hoarded all your life. Letting go of this is a way to create strength through vulnerability.

Step 5 *"Admit to God, to ourselves and to another human being the exact nature of our wrongs."* This is where the beauty begins. Sharing your inventory with another person, someone you trust, allows you not to hide or run away anymore. We face our truths and we turn the incomprehensibly demoralizing secrets into power by giving it no power over our life anymore. I have worked the steps three times and have shared my secrets with several sponsors in various stages of my addiction. This has allowed me to release the painful past and shame that came with my actions and hurtful things I was doing to myself and others in private. Release is cathartic in the healing process. Going through the steps over again allowed me to go back in time and have empathy and compassion for my parents.

It was a long and slow process to accept my problem with alcoholism. After spending some time back in the program, several large groups asked me to speak publicly at meetings. I shared my story, my experience, my strength and my hope. Part of me was hesitant but was proud of my progress and recovery. Groups wrote to me from all over California to ask me to share my story about self-care within corporate burnout situations as a motivational speaker. I volunteered my time and made countless trips to speak at many venues and delivered evidence that recovery works.

I received a new high, "a spiritual high", from speaking at university campuses, high schools, recovery homes, half-way houses, women's shelters, juvenile hall detention centers, detox treatment facilities, church group luncheons, women's networking groups and corporate knowledge session environments. I also spoke at hospitals and institutions for people who were not able to attend outside meetings. These were the first of many speaking engagements where I shared my testimony with others to let others know there is hope. Most importantly, I rigorously worked the program more for healing and experience to share at a deeper level.

Each time I left a facility, my heart was filled with so much gratitude. Gratitude for a second chance to live. Sharing my story allowed me to remember where I came from and to see the miracle of recovery and growth in myself. Having a positive impact on others gave me a renewed sense of hope and purpose. I knew I was walking into my Soul path, calling, and purpose.

I am a Healer.
I am a Survivor.
I am an Awakener.

There are no words to describe the feeling when someone gets their first day or year token (*recovery chip*). I've been there many times in the past and understand the suffering, pain and hopelessness. I knew that life would get better if I continued to keep the faith.

> *"As I continued to keep coming back, I got a broader view of who I am, and I know I had to give it away to keep it. I am responsible."* —**Journal entry**, *July 5, 2019*

As a parent, when I left the youth lockdown facility, I was reminded to work hard to raise my son right, so he never experienced what those less fortunate children had gone through. Today, I can share the miracle of recovery with my son through working the program and practicing the principles every day. My little family also reaps the benefits of healing, as well.

Here are some of the valuable tools I've learned from working the steps of the program:

- *Being honest with myself and others allowed me to live with integrity and have a clear conscience;*
- *I am free to be me by gaining a deeper understanding of who I am by working the steps;*

- *Deep prayer and meditation practices keep the soul grounded and awake;*
- *Struggles will always be a part of life and I am able to overcome and cope with extra tools in my toolbox;*
- *Journaling your personal inventory, "grudge lists ", allows you to grow as a human being;*
- *Making amends to those you've hurt, apologizing and getting closure feels good.*

Recovery taught me how to take care of myself and show others that it is possible to recover from a hopeless state of mind. Everything starts from your mindset.

Sharing my story to help others is the main reason why I gave up my precious anonymity when I entered into the world of public speaking.

It has taken me great faith and sheer strength to be an avowed Asian woman in recovery. I am humbled and proud to see the growing numbers of those in recovery who dare to share their story and support those who are suffering. Sharing means we no longer suffer alone in our disease.

Things moved and shifted for me as I became more my authentic self. I received an outpouring of letters, text messages and emails from family, friends, students, men and women seeking comfort and advice to help them in their addiction with codependency, sex, love, drugs and alcohol.

Today, I continue to take a personal inventory of myself. I continue to gather the knowledge I learn about myself, inside and outside the recovery rooms. This gives me the power to influence my life in the most positive and productive ways.

I am finally living a life beyond my wildest dreams.

I have had a spiritual awakening and I am putting all that I've learned to good use. Being spiritually awake and moving at a slow and steady pace in life allows me to gain control of my future.

What I have learned has shaped the person I've become today.

REFLECTIONS ON THE 12 STEPS

"Moderate in order to taste the joys of life in abundance." —**Epicurus**

Being a recovering addict of all sorts I realize the most dangerous thing is to stop working the program in its entirety. When working with others, I am reminded of the silent but deadly truth of addiction and its consequences. I am grateful for my recovery, and I feel blessed to be able to carry on the message and traditions with others in my life. It's a healthy lifestyle and way of living. Here are some of my personal perspectives of the pros and cons from the program.

Step 1 - "We admitted we were powerless over X and that our lives had become unmanageable."

Pro: Admitting complete defeat to addiction and hitting rock bottom was not easy. Still, the program proved it worked by offering a consistent support system of love, commitment and compassion – genuine care and understanding from the community was the key to my success. I didn't feel like I was alone, as the community understood what I was feeling and how I was struggling.

Con: Letting go of the drink was easy, but emotional dependency was a hard fact and still prevalent in my life. One single program alone didn't solve the cross addictions of codependency, lack of boundaries in relationships and my low self-esteem issues. I continued to act out in these areas until I was willing to let go of toxic people, places and things.

Step 2 - "We Come to believe that a Power greater than ourselves could restore us to sanity."

Pro: Believing in a power greater than me helped restore me to sanity. I struggled with isolation and control all my life and I finally asked for help.

Con: I grew up as a Buddhist and had a hard time grasping the concept of God. Ultimately I grew closer to my Higher Power over the years and recognized his loving fingerprints throughout my life. I began to believe, as I saw how the presence of God worked in other peoples' lives.

Step 3 - *"Made a decision to turn our will and our lives over to the care of God as we understand Him."*

Pro: As I decided to turn my life over to a Higher Power, my life began to change miraculously. I was no longer chasing the high and learned to be still to allow God to work in my life. I got through challenges, one day at a time, as I continued to turn my will over.

Con: Turning my life and will over to God daily was hard, but I knew what the consequences would be if I didn't keep my higher power first. I'm grateful for what I've learned. I no longer turn my back on God and I have taken back the control and living my will.

Step 4 - "Make a searching and fearless moral inventory of ourselves."

Pro: Writing out a "grudge list" of demoralizing things I had done to myself and others was hard, but by identifying the root of the problem, I was able to gain a deep level of awareness of who I was and how I behaved all these years. Understanding the character defects that were holding me back and limiting my belief system was key to my recovery.

Con: The hard part was to reach back into my memory for all the bad things that had happened to me in my life that I wasn't ready to look at yet. Looking at resentments, fears, grudges and personal sexual inventory was not natural, but I ultimately pushed through the pain of looking at my part in all of it.

Step 5 - "Admitted to God, to ourselves and to another human being the exact nature of our wrongs.

Pro: This step was special. After writing my inventory, I released all my fears and innermost secrets to another person and it lifted all the hurt and pain that scarred me. It has been a beautiful process and I'm blessed to be able to support other women in their recovery and give back the love that was so generously given to me.

Con: Unfortunately, with the trust issues I've had since I was a young girl, I jumped from one relationship with a sponsor to another. I was continuously searching for answers in each one. I was not able to be as thorough as I wanted to be until recently. I did the program my way and struggled many years because I was never emotionally sober in my relationships.

Step 6 – "*We are entirely ready to have God remove all these defects of character.*

Pro: Once I completed a 4th step inventory and shared all my painful hidden secrets with my sponsor, I was free from the shame and guilt that I buried in my subconscious mind. Intellectually, I knew I was ready during my last emotional rock bottom and I was in enough pain to ask God to remove these defects. I was not able to do it for myself.

Con: Looking at the defects of character on a daily basis is hard because there is no reprieve. Once you come into the program, you don't become cured and there is no graduation date. You must continue to remain current and recognize that you still have these traits. The only difference today is that I review my behavior and actions on a daily basis to ensure I'm emotionally stable and sober.

Step 7 "*Humbly ask Him to remove our shortcomings.*"

Pro: In this step I turned my will over to the care of God and humbly asked him to remove my defective characteristics. I understood that humility was not humiliation. I started to let go of my character defects to heal.

Con: When I was in active addiction, it was hard to see and recognize the areas I needed help with. It took a long time to uncover the character defects, therefore it took a long time to get right-sized.

Step 8 – "*Make a list of all persons we harmed and become willing to make amends to them all.*"

Pro: Through this step, I identified people in my life that I had to make amends to. I came to realize there were a lot of people that I hurt. I also realized that there was a lot of hope knowing I was able to clean up the past.

Con: Looking at this amends list was not easy and took a long time to get to acceptance that I owed them amends. This process took a lot of self-reflection.

Step 9 – "*Make direct amends to such people wherever possible, except when to do so would injure them or others.*"

Pro: I was able to clear up the wreckage of my past and come to terms with it. Also, I cleared up my mind so I did not make the same mistake again. Once you get to this step, life becomes real and you recognize the hurt and pain you've caused. This step helps you clean your past up. Even though it's a hard step, it's a fruitful one.

Con: There were some people that I haven't been able to find to make amends to them.

Step 10 – "*Continue to take a personal inventory and when wrong, promptly admit it.*"

Pro: I took my personal inventory on a daily basis and learned to admit my wrongs. I had a higher level of self-awareness and kept my side of the street clean daily.

Con: It's hard to keep up with the daily hustle and bustle and make time for yourself. This step requires daily journaling and reflection to stay current. Thank goodness I practice self-care regularly to make time for myself.

Step 11 – Seek through prayer and meditation to improve your conscious contact with God *as you understand Him*, praying only for knowledge of His will over us and the power to carry that out.

Pro: I sought God through prayer and meditation to improve my connection to my higher power daily. The knowledge I learned in those rooms gave me the ability to influence my life in the most positive and productive ways. I use the tools in my life and now live a life beyond my wildest dreams!

Step 12 – *"Having had a spiritual awakening as the result of these steps, try to carry this message to alcoholics and to practice these principles in all our affairs."*

> **Pro:** I feel as though I have been spiritually awake for a long time, however it was only once I was working all the steps that I knew what path to take. Whether it was right or wrong, I gained a lot of experience in all areas of my life and finally was able to pass along the message of hope to others because I was doing the work.
>
> **Con:** Unfortunately, any kind of addiction is so hard to kick because those crutches and old habits were what we used to survive. I didn't have healthy boundaries with myself as it related to relationships. I was spiritually awake at this step, but I kept going back into bondage and wasn't sharing the message to others because I was ashamed of all my relapses.

"I am uncovering and shedding light on a lot of darkness in my life. Even though I've tried to process it before, I am now truly understanding my weaknesses at a whole deeper level of meaning. I'm humbled. It's amazing what happens when you don't give up on yourself."
—Journal entry, *July 12, 2017*

Being a sober individual has so many benefits, but none more so than the ability to grow upwards, experience and see the good not only in the world – but inside your own body, heart and soul. Here are just a few that blew my mind about being sober to inspire you...

- *Sobriety helps you be more confident and stable.*
- *Sobriety helps you admit your mistakes and try to be a better person, every day.*
- *Sobriety helps you help individuals around you and receive gifts in return.*

- *Sobriety helps you experience joy – honest to goodness joy that comes from the most surprising of places. (I love the feeling of opening my eyes in the morning, awake and aware of what the day holds in store.)*
- *Sobriety helps you feel the energy of the Universe around you – being in active addiction keeps you distracted, numb and disconnected from the spirit of the light, but sobriety brings feelings of unbelievable potential.*

>> Are you ready to dive in deeper and find out how you can overcome your past and make your present better than you ever could have imagined?

OVERCOMING LOSS AND REGRET

"Sometimes, we're so concerned about giving our children what we never had growing up, we neglect to give them what we did have growing up." —**James Dobson**

My son has been a pivotal part of my growth and truly saved my life when he came into this world in 2008. I was tired, broken and had very little hope. Suddenly a precious face looked right back at me. From that Moment, I was reborn. He saved my broken heart and put the pieces before all the trauma back together again.

His innocence gave me purpose and hope.

I wish I could tell you it happened just that suddenly – that single Moment when I cradled his face in my hands that everything was different, but every parent knows it's a lot more complicated than that.

I've lived many lives in this one – (sometimes, I like to joke that *"dog years have nothing on the sheer multitude of days, hours and Moments I've breathed in and out."*) Noah's birth was one of many, *"starting over"* points for me. I feel so deeply for my son. I love him just so much. In return, he gives me so much joy – we always find ourselves coming back to each other with hugs and kisses. He looks a lot like me, although I see other people in him – his grandfather, his father and the many individuals that have come before. His soul is embedded with depth, grace and unconditional love.

On the evening of Noah's 8th birthday, I noticed that his body had changed. His mid drift was bulging, his arms were no longer defined, and he was 10 pounds heavier than the last time he weighed himself. As his mother, I was disappointed I was missing parts of him growing and changing. I felt like I was doing the best to support his growth in healthy ways, however I had failed him at some level. We addressed this concern and made a conscious decision to support one another going into the New Year to eat healthier – to support his growing body as well.

We took a dry erase marker to his mirror and drafted an action plan to help him grow big and strong. "*But Mom*!" he said with his knowing grin, *"we're missing something important: Social Media! You're going off social media."* That was the first real *"Social media cleanse"* I did. We called this the *"Big Cleanse"* where we detoxed off Facebook, Instagram, Twitter and YouTube.

He officially shut down my operating system.

Noah said to me. *"Mom, it's been on my bucket list to get you off social media since I was five years old."* That was a powerful Moment for me, one that made me realize: Technology had overtaken the Moments I should be parenting. At that Moment, I realized Noah's sudden weight gain was the result of child neglect and abandonment. I was abandoning my son and made the realization that I had also abandoned myself. I was reaching for things outside of me to make me feel better.

I broke down and cried.

Social media has wrecked my life in a lot of ways. If it weren't for my son, I wouldn't have realized the harmful impact that it had in my life. I used social media and other things as a crutch, and it served me precisely what I thought I needed:

Distraction. Escapism. Diversion.

Addiction is very sneaky.

Noah's mission was to shut down my "*Operating System,*" he explained joyfully. We initially agreed to stay off our phones and gadgets for one week, but the social media detox lasted for twelve weeks.

> *"I gave him my undivided attention and he became more of the Noah I knew was in there. Self-awareness set in for him, too."*
> **—Journal entry**, *June 26, 2017*

PART THREE

AWAKENING YOUR GROWTH

CHAPTER SEVEN

THE HAVENING METHOD

"Teaching is the highest form of understanding.' —**Aristotle**

The Havening Technique gave me the tools to stay in the present Moment. This helped me slow down and spend time with my son. We experienced incredible breakthroughs. The truth is: I had been blinded and suffering from my work-life and social media distractions.

My son helped me connect the dots.

We experienced a lot of breakthroughs during our social media cleanse. One night after going out to eat, we came home and he asked me, *"Why does this feel like a dream, Mommy?"* Noah was finally so happy. And honestly – it did feel like a dream. We hadn't connected with one another this close for as long as I can remember. That night Noah and I spent the evening focusing and practicing visualization and manifestation techniques. He visualized zip-lining down Big Bear Mountain, strong and confident.

We use the technique to help create what we desire. Havening or any visualization tools is not always about reaching to the past, but you can create the future self. For Noah, it was merely to have fun with his Mom.

I made the call to the zip-line company the next day and we made it happen – next thing you know we're up in the mountains at Big Bear, zip-lining!

The trip was a success, not just because we shared the Moment, but more so because I had been missing out because I was consumed with my fast-paced lifestyle. The so-called "work-life balance" was nearly non-existent.

With this particular Havening technique, Noah also wasn't scared or nervous being up high. Havening gave him the confidence to visualize his success. I realized at that Moment how powerful the tool was and how much I wanted to practice it in my coaching business. We have experienced many profound breakthroughs and *"A-Ha! Moments"* together once we stopped being glued to our phones. Living life outside the digital vortex is mind-blowing. Every parent and everyone should practice staying off social media, off their phones and other gadgets that cause distraction.

Practice this *"Slow Down"* tool of being social media, technology and phone-free and see what happens when you stay present with your loved ones and those relevant to you without outside distractions.

WHAT IS HAVENING?

"And the day came when the risk to remain tight in a bud was more painful than the risk it took to blossom." —**Anais Nin**

Among all the unique therapeutic techniques I have tried to bring my anxiety down, Havening has been one of the most helpful and therapeutic techniques. Havening is able to bring my anxiety down to a manageable level. Learning about this technique through my therapist, Dr. Kate Truitt, changed my life.

"Havening Techniques (Havening), is a method, which is designed to change the brain to de-traumatize the memory and remove its negative effects from both our psyche and body," as referenced on the www.havening.org website. The process of the Havening Technique requires touch and breathing exercises to help reduce anxiety and stress. "Havening", is an innovative healing approach developed and created by Ronald Ruden, MD, PhD in collaboration with his brother Steven Ruden, DDS.

Havening came from extensive experience and research on psycho-sensory therapy. *"This healing modality uses the foundation of neuroscience and neurobiology, which uses sensory input to alter thought, mood and behavior,"* (Reference: www.havening.org). When an event or experience is perceived as traumatic or stressful, it becomes encoded and changes your life as the event is stuck permanently in the psyche and the body, often with life-altering consequences. Unfortunately these traumatic experiences for me manifested as recurring dialogue full of negativity, fear and painful events that I was not able to directly "*get over*" or "*shake off.*"

This method has been very effective in helping me heal from my personal past traumas and the negative recurring thoughts that the trauma elicits when thinking about my past. It is a healing modality I use to relieve emotional disturbance, wellness and stress management and perform at my peak state.

Havening includes touch as a therapeutic tool and I have personally experienced first-hand the emotional, mental and physical health benefits during my therapy sessions with Dr. Truitt.

Havening is a personal journey. I've discovered so much about myself through the training process for the certification, personal uses as well as sharing it with others in my life. The way Havening works is that it allows serotonin to increase naturally as each individual feels safe to talk about specific topics. "Havening, the transitive verb of the word haven, means to put into a safe place." (Reference: www.havening.org). I have performed over 15 Havening case studies and have helped friends and family with their stuck emotions through times of stress.

At the beginning of each Havening case study session, we talk through and uncover a stuck emotional (big or mini traumas) time frame in the person's past. In this way, we can identify what they need the most help with and ask them to identify a specific body sensation that surfaces from a traumatic experience. I ask them to go into their body and describe what they are feeling and if any thoughts are more dominant than others. It's a challenging process and a delicate process that encapsulates so much of the past – acted out in dreams and body actions. It's been a wonderful journey to help others overcome their past whether it be with Havening, my coaching business or counseling sessions to help guide and offer help with this amazing healing modality. It works!

REAL-WORLD USES OF HAVENING

"The fault, dear Brutus, is not in our stars but in ourselves."
—William Shakespeare, Julius Caesar

I've personally struggled with post-traumatic stress disorder (PTSD), trauma, depression, anxiety and a variation of mental breakdowns. I have practiced Self-Havening on myself numerous occasions. Havening allowed me to bring down stress and helped me through panic attacks. I have been able to escape the inescapable situations in my subconscious mind. The worst fears I had growing up were the ones I wasn't able to escape from – but for me now, that's not a problem anymore. I've learned to soothe myself and practice self-love by being gentle with myself when recurring negative thoughts surface again.

Here's an example. You are climbing up a mountain and your foot slips. You topple over and you are thousands of feet up in the air dangling 5,000 feet above ground from a single rope. Let's say you were able to escape danger. However, you now suffer from post-traumatic stress from the event. You arrive at the therapist and seemingly can't seem to get the fear of the 5,000 feet drop out of your mind. You have constant flashbacks of falling to the ground and succumbing to your death. In this case, you get diagnosed with PTSD. You get lost and keep cycling through what may have happened, or how you felt during the trauma. You are not alone. So many people play a tape of injury over and over in their heads and they start to think they might be insane.

There is real fear joined with a tremendous consequence: Slipping farther or letting go might mean death. Havening can fix the inescapable fear only you experienced and only you have memories of. Our brains are very funny, miraculous muscles that retain memories for a long time. Through Havening, you remove the sensory memory that is associated with fall. You will now be able to continue to make climbs without the pre-conditioned fear related to the dismay of slipping and falling to your death.

The reality is – the Moment that trauma happened was buried so far down into the psyche; it needed some assistance to become "unstuck" and cycled-through. Havening tackles both the "*what's happened*" and the "*what-ifs*". Havening helps permanently encode a new thought process and quickly rewires your thinking within several sessions.

EVEN ATHLETES USE IT

"It is in your moments of decision that your destiny is shaped."
—Tony Robbins

During my training for the Havening certification, there was a case study of a well-known athlete on a famous football team who suffered PTSD after being in a near-death experience at the hands of an armed robber at an ATM in broad daylight. For months, he was unable to get onto the football field because of the PTSD and felt continuously triggered by the event.

By the time he arrived at the therapist's office, he was traumatized from the event. He was fearful all the time. During the incident, the assailant, who almost took his life, was shot by a security guard Moments after a gun was pointed two inches from the athlete's face during this robbery. During the same time frame, there were people across the street enjoying themselves for lunch at a restaurant unaware of the situation that was unfolding, which also caused him to later be fearful of walking into safe establishments as well.

What happens in the brain when a person has been faced with a situation where their life is at stake, their reptilian "*Lizard Brain*" goes into fight or flight mode. Fear is actually associated with our senses. What we see, hear, feel, smell or touch gets encoded into our amygdala ("Amy" for short) and that association can be of positive or negative form. Our senses are powerful and can easily be turned into a trigger with PTSD. There is also what is known as complex-PTSD caused by a series of traumatic events or prolonged one. Things that are happening around us during the time the event occurred can cause recurring triggers. Sight, sound and smell associated with these incidents are usually the most dominant. Either one can trigger or cause the memory feedback loop to continue to stay stuck with the traumatic event.

The athlete described above continued to feel helpless and experienced such fear from this experience for months. He was unable to figure out where the continuous anxiety and triggers came from. Still, through working with the therapist and the process of Havening, he was able to recall the assailant wearing a red t-shirt and through this, he realized that seeing red shirts was an unconscious trigger he attached to his football team's jersey.

With the help of the therapist, he identified the trigger, re-encoded his feelings and memory recall. Identifying the source of the trigger is critical in this process. The "*Red Shirt*" was the source of the traumatic event.

My clarinet I carried with me on the day of the sexual assault equated to the *"Red-Shirt"* of the athlete. *It was my post traumatic trigger, a reminder of a bad thing that happened in my life.*

For me, through Havening, I realized I had a disassociation with music for years, especially being in band during my high school years after being raped in sophomore year by a complete stranger. The memory association during that time frame from the past haunted me for a long time. In addition to the feelings of guilt and shame for years because I ditched school that day to see a boyfriend, but also because I was picked up by a stranger who was very spiritually sick.

Sadly, I didn't talk about myself for years. I never wanted people to ask me about myself. I didn't really know the person I was in high school. But more importantly, I didn't want anyone to know how insecure, remorseful, angry and shameful I felt about myself. I blacked out that day and blocked out that part of my life. After years of therapy and Havening, I finally remembered that my "*Red Shirt*" trigger was my clarinet associated with music because it was my excuse to be out early and it was with me the entire morning of the rape.

I finally figured out why I had acted out so much throughout my life. I lived life as if bad things didn't happen. I suppressed bad feelings. I detached from everyone and everything that seemed to be a potential threat and became hyper aware of predators. I picked up the habit of escaping from people, places and things when I stopped feeling safe. I ran away emotionally, physically and spiritually before anyone could get to know me. Yes, I did live recklessly, but now I know why. That's the difference. It was not my fault completely but I finally took responsibility for everything.

"After years in therapy and understanding what was going on in my mind with all the trauma, I prayed for him, I forgave my attacker and finally moved on." —**Journal entry** *June 20, 2019*

WAIT... IS HAVENING THE ONLY WAY TO SLOW DOWN?

"It is the same with people as it is with riding a bicycle. Only when moving can one comfortably maintain one's balance."
—Albert Einstein- In a letter to son, Eduard, Feb 5, 1930.

There have been so many ways I've tried to eliminate toxic, energy-sucking habits from my life. These habits need to be erased to live a happy, calm and healthy life. While I believe whole-heartedly in Havening, there are MANY ways we can eliminate toxicity, non-productive thoughts, take action with our lives and help us get to a place of peace. In Chapter Eight, we'll explore new ways to detach old memories and rise to the occasion of your new life!

>> **Ready? Let's Get Going...**

CHAPTER EIGHT

SLOW DOWN AND ENJOY LIFE

"No matter what people tell you, words and ideas, can change the world."
—Robin Williams

"What you seek is seeking you." **—Rumi**

L*isten up!* Tomorrow is not guaranteed. No one knows how much time we have left. We need to be intentional and live life fully with the only thing we have, which is today. If you picked up this book – you are probably o*verworked, burned out, burning out, fatigued, stressed, have a chronic illness*, or are *daydreaming* of a vacation that *never* seems to happen. We need to slow down and enjoy life. My friend and mentor, also named Cathy, with over thirty years of recovery in her sweet and loving voice always says to me, "*Stop and smell the roses, Miss Cathy.*"

To stop and smell the roses is to take time to enjoy the finer and enjoyable things in life. Truly appreciate each present Moment. It's especially important when we are overly stressed and burned out to take time out of our busy schedule and enjoy the beauty of life or things that matter to us the most.

Many of us only *"look"* at the rose. We rarely ever stop to smell them. I rarely remember myself thoroughly enjoying roses I've been given or have received by taking time to enjoy their aroma. Next time when you're in a grocery store or buying flowers or roses, stop and take a deep breath in with your nose and all its scent to embed itself into your heart. It is a gift to smell their natural soothing fragrances, as well as touch them to feel the beauty in their satiny petals. Similarly, don't just go through life with only responsibilities and work, but take time to appreciate and pursue your true passions and Soul callings. Your Soul purpose becomes more evident when you tune in to listen to what your heart is yearning and what is guiding you within.

Truly experience it by walking on your Soul's path so your life becomes richer.

SLOW DOWN THE BLAME GAME

"The most powerful words in the Universe are the words you say to yourself." —**Marie Forleo**

For many years, I was in a rut. I had concerned myself with things I had no business worrying about. I buried myself deep in the hole of depression. I was tuning into uninspiring dialogue and added extra outside noise, unhealthy distractions, mindless bantering, worrying about financial futures and disempowering political news. I became unbalanced and felt depressed often. I self-diagnosed it as depression, fear, self-doubt, low self-esteem, isolation, relationship anorexia, insecurity, a manic episode and even being a bit crazy at times.

Sometimes it was just better to blame other people. I played a perfect *"Blame Game."* After a while, my reality became so confusing and detached. After blaming another person for so long, I forgot who even started the fight. *Isn't that the truth!* The negative inner dialogue got worse. It became exhausting. I was so tired of being tired of beating myself up. I finally had to decide to *let go and let God.* Eventually with practice over time it became a more natural way to live.

Forgiveness allowed me to let go of resentments. Self-care allowed me to let go of self-abandonment and self-abuse. Writing this book helped me with shifting my mindset and helped me claw out of the hole of what was once a pitiful and incomprehensible demoralizing existence.

The ride was excruciatingly painful and hard at times, but worth every minute. Every tear shed was worth it. I would re-live each minute of my painful past to have my son again precisely the way he is today. That would be the only way to have this story to share with you.

"I would do it again in a heartbeat to find the unconditional love I've been searching for all my life – the passion within me. To find the love of my life, every inch of me."
—**Journal entry**, *February, 14, 2019*

We all have dreams, but we usually don't dare to dream them because we get stuck in ruts mentioned earlier. "*The work rut.*" "*The parenthood rut.*" "*The emotional rut.*" "*The physically drained-out rut.*" The dreaded *"Rat-race" rut.* It was mind boggling to me how hard it was to pull myself out of these ruts even after I thought I had experienced a spiritual awakening, a Moment of enlightenment with super inspiration and hyper awareness pumping through my veins. It was definitely game over when I lacked self-motivation, self-worth or any type of will power. Throw in a kid, a mortgage, an uninspiring career, a few ill family members and self-confidence certainly can roll down the wrong hill.

The lingering self-doubt caused me to be in a constant state of fear, which stopped the state of flow dead in its tracks. I have spent the past twenty years sitting in about twenty cubicles working in corporate America, hustling and bustling, dialing for dollars, trying my best to life hack the "*Secret of Success.*" By examining other people and my own work ethic, I came to the conclusion that the so-called "*American dream*" was living in the hectic, fast lane.

The only way out was to work harder and faster to get there sooner. *Wherever there was?* I was working hard at a job from 9 to 5, commuting 40 miles, weaving in and out of Southern California traffic jams. Suiting up and showing up for work even when life was excruciatingly painful. Racing home to cram in school work in the late hours of the night, just to go right back to the grind the next day. Yeah, we're living the life…the grand master plan of a life called "*The American Dream.*" Slowing down was never around the corner.

We become robots working in the infamous fast- paced, dynamic work/life culture and balanced on the dream called *"Life"*. This lifestyle became a part of my Asian-American DNA. Secretly and slowly it took a toll on my mental, physical, emotional health and state of mind. Corporate burnout was sitting there waiting for me. Burnout affects everyone I know at some level. Occupational burnout just sits there patiently waiting for us to succumb to its trap and seize another victim. It patiently waits for us to throw our hands up in the air and wave the white flag. If we're not careful as a society, it sits there waiting with masks ready for us to use for fear of catching a viruses and dis-ease.

"Slowing down quiets the mind so you can ease into a Beautiful Existence!
—Journal entry, March 31, 2020

For years, this was the only life I knew living in America, the land of the free and great land of opportunity. I didn't know any other way. The harder you work, the more you'll be rewarded and get your goals done quicker. Capitalism can be a toxic pill leaving you constantly chasing the dangling carrot. We become hamsters forever running feverishly on the wheels of the capitalist system, chasing dreams and competing with each other. You work your tail off, earn a decent income and the reward is to earn a great life "*They said*" – whoever *"they"* were?

The only problem is that we forget to take care of ourselves, our health, take a break, until it's too late. Unfortunately the majority of this wisdom and training was handed down by our ancestors, parents, friends, peers and leaders, but I didn't always integrate it into my life.

THE BIG HUSTLE

"Good things happen to those who hustle." —**Anais Nin**

When I was 14, I worked as a front office assistant at an Asian family-owned orthodontist office. At that job, I learned how to use proper manners with patients; otherwise, I wouldn't fit the mold of a polite young Asian teenager.

However, by the age of fifteen, the big hustle was on. I was armed with a worker's permit and worked as a busgirl clearing dirty tables at a Country Harvest Buffet. At that job, I learned to move dirty plates off tables as fast as I could with a positive attitude and smile! One evening I earned a crisp 50 dollar tip for a large dinner party of fifty. The lesson I learned that evening was hard work equaled making money and the wild chase was on!

As soon as I got behind a cordless headset phone dialer at my first telemarketing job at 16 years old selling fraud credit protection services, *it truly was on*! The actress in me came out. I became the author of my life and the virtual world became my stage. I was able to use my charm, wit and conversational skills to earn a living.

At some point on my journey, I became highly spiritual and followed my astrology stars! Based on my sign born under the year of a fire snake, I have been told that luck in the form of money and business would come to me. The work I do today as a recruiter is incredibly rewarding financially and socially. I drifted in and out of reality, daydreamed a bunch and forgot about essential things in life. Things like taking care of myself and taking vacations were non-existent.

I spent the past twenty years cultivating my craft and earned a great living with the "*gift of gab*." But not only was it a great asset, but it also helped me launch me into the great state of misery as well. I talked my way into exhaustion, became a people pleaser and lacked boundaries in all my affairs. My passion and zest for life, along with a long list of addictive behaviors, transformed me into a workaholic and I sacrificed my health and vitality – as previously mentioned in the Chapter 2 called "Workaholism".

I worked hard, just like both my parents. I didn't often take time off, go on vacation, relax, or practice healthy behaviors to take care of myself, nor did I stop to smell the roses. Taking vacation time and slowing down the pace of my life was a hard concept for me to swallow as someone used to going on fast turbo mode. It was almost a thing at work when I was working in a corporate setting to be nervous to ask for time off even when I earned it. Back when I worked in the office, I don't recall any managers nudging or urging any of us to go on vacation. I remember always feeling guilty, scared and fearful of losing the valuable time to find the next candidate or win a new client.

Even though my career is one of my greatest joys in life, I realize now that work isn't my entire life. I am not saying that you should abandon your job and responsibilities. I am recommending that you practice self-care and self-love in that work-life balance, first and foremost.

After going through cancer treatment in 2018 and hitting another bottom emotionally, I started taking time off and focusing on the important things in life. It has changed my entire Universe, inside out. Cancer changed my perspective on life. It rocked me to my core. I finally gave myself permission to take it easy, relax, slow down and truly appreciate being *alive.* Life is so precious and too short all in the same breath. Your life can change within a blink of an eye. Car accidents, broken bones, emergency visits, cancer diagnosis, pink slips at work, deaths, breakups, emotional breakdowns, bipolar manic episodes and then *boom* there it all goes down the drain again. It's so easy to slip into old unhealthy, toxic patterns of behaviors.

The completion of this book was partially inspired by another evening of mindlessly scrolling and grinding through Linkedin one night at 1:00 am, trying to catch up on the latest trending posts. Usually while holding my breath and a dim glimmer of hope in the search for something inspirational to help launch my spirit into yet another stressful workday. This daunting, but effective method was usually followed by the osmosis of a chaotic mental chatter that manifested itself into low self-esteem, judgmental behavior and obsessive comparison of one profile after the next and the sheer panic for fear of falling behind in life in general.

Does this sound familiar?

Generally, by the end of the 2nd hour, I'm physically exhausted, emotionally drained, mentally debilitated, but yet I somehow manage to hone into my next best target client or possible recruit. Usually, I could find a burned-out employee ready to take a leap of faith to the darker side.

By 2:15 am, I ran across a post written by a 2nd connection, who wrote about her brother-in-law who just died at the age of 46 from a heart attack. His funeral was that day. He was a hardworking, successful, dedicated father, husband and employee of a major corporation. She wrote the post, not seeking condolences or even prayers, but the post was almost written like a public service announcement to heed a friendly reminder to warn people of the dangers of working hard and pushing yourself to the limits. She was saying enjoy your life, don't kill yourself with a reminder to "SLOW DOWN!" *Slow down and don't die with unused vacation days* is what I got from what she said.

Linkedin is a platform filled with high achievers, entrepreneurs, hustlers, gurus and those who want to go faster and get more done. I know this first hand because I am a passionate, hardworking, play-hard, go-get-em', zest-for-life professional *social media junkie.* In other words, an addicted workaholic caught up in the fast lanes online and offline, who doesn't go on enough vacations.

I worked hard 50-60 hours a week in a corporate setting for many years. I confused high volume activity with productivity. Working hard was supposed to equal results. I didn't make time to care for my health, plan fun trips, hang out with friends, or stay in contact with my family. Sometimes, I forgot that prayer, meditation, journaling and practicing mindfulness was necessary during long work hours as a way to help minimize corporate burnout.

Slowing down was the answer. Inaction or slowing down was the only action that made a difference between happiness and burning out, between failure and success.

As I was trying my best to learn how to slow down, I miscalculated my efforts. In 2018, I ignored neck and shoulder pain that turned out to be cancer. This diagnosis forced me to slow my life down and forced me to take a more in-depth look at what was happening in my life. Slowing down helped me build a foundation for success in my life.

By 2:45 am, I shut my phone down, swung open my laptop and began the final chapter of my "*Book Thing.*" What started with the intention of writing the final chapter of my book ended up being this chapter you're reading now! It has been the best chapter of my life to finally get to the finish line of getting the book done. "*SLOW DOWN – Mastering the Art Slowing Down into A Beautiful Existence*" has been my motto nowadays and a personal manifesto to help others on their journey to living an extraordinary life. One that I can appreciate every minute, but also one I didn't even know existed for me.

Life is too short. Celebrate each day. Make the best of it while you're here. Just because our bodies can be pushed to the limits so hard doesn't mean we should. Remember to take care of your health – physically, mentally, emotionally and spiritually. Go on vacation. Or better yet, take a "*Spiritual Vacation*" as a better way of thinking about the way you live your life. I've been on this spiritual vacation each day. I appreciate each breath and every morning I wake up. I am so grateful to have this chance to write and share my love with the world.

"Writing this book was not only cathartic, but it has helped heal all the broken parts of me in ways I never imagined."
—**Journal entry**, *February 20, 2020*

I'm so grateful that late-night Linkedin post gave me the inspiration to complete the book. I've been working on this book project for a very long time. I have to admit I was dealing with low vibrating nonsensical chaos, self-esteem issues, self-loathing and self-diminishing issues that stemmed from years of not taking care of me. I obsessed with other things and did not focus on slowing down. I had every excuse not to get this book to the finish line, but this is it. I focused on finishing it in 2020, no matter what.

Here were some not-so inspiring recurring negative self-talk dialogue and excuses that continued to come up when I was writing the book. Hope this helps you knowing that it occurs with me as well:

- *I have no time;*
- *I'm not good enough;*
- *I am so unorganized;*

- *I have so much work to do;*
- *It's not perfect;*
- *Something is wrong with me.*

With mental chatter like this, no one would be able to get anything done. We all should go on a vacation and just relax! Between personal coaches, social media influencers and corporate leaders – they tout a fast-paced and dynamic work culture. This modern world we live in can be overstimulating and pushes us to function like robots. What I discovered was that I need to slow down despite what the corporate "experts" were saying.

Health, wealth, love and connectivity are the four critical areas in life that can help you succeed in creating a life you love in business and personal relationships. If you are able to master these four areas, you will be able to enjoy a more profound sense of fulfillment. These areas require balance and goal setting. In my coaching business, I use a simplified quadrant to help set short and long-term goals and to help eliminate excessive overthinking. I look forward to sharing these life strategies with you.

>> Are you ready to create the life you love and live beyond your wildest dreams?

CHAPTER NINE

CREATING YOUR DREAM LIFE

"Success is most often achieved by those who don't know that failure is inevitable." —**Coco Chanel**

In 2016, I partnered up with a coach with Inner Access Coaching programs. I met my coach, Superwoman, through attending a T. Harv Ecker *"Millionaire Mind Intensive"* program. I began the transformational process to become a richer me! With my coach, we focused on and worked on four areas of my life. The four areas were: health & fitness, finances, relationships and dream goals (some call it a passion project).

Under my *'Dream Goals',* I visualized and wrote down a goal of writing and publishing a book one day. Writing and getting the book to the finish line was one of the biggest mountains I have ever climbed, but the most rewarding goal I have ever accomplished.

This completion of this book felt like the most beautiful piece of artwork completed by an artist that finally got hung on a favorite wall in their home. A lot of time, sweat and tears poured into the pages of this book with sheer persistency to finish it. It was tough, but most importantly, I *never* gave up. With sheer grit, I kept going and going. Writing and writing. I talked about the *Book Thing* for years and faced every emotion known going through the process. At times there was a lot of fear, shame, heartache, embarrassment and pain, but at the same time and in the end I gained so much joy, peace and love in my heart each step of the way. I would encourage each one of you to never stop pursuing your dreams and list your passion projects down. Like Tony Robbin's say, if its' not written down or not on your calendar – it doesn't exist.

A part of the program was to declutter different areas of my life.

Purging, clearing and cleansing became a weekly routine. The only problem I had was the more clarity I had in my life, the more I was forced to work, rework and refocus the book so many times.

When I was diagnosed with cancer, the recommendation was to just stop, slow down and focus on my health. Over and over I was told, *"Get through the surgery! And then come back when you're ready."* With so much on my plate from medical treatments, doctors' appointments, work, raising a child and outside noise, it definitely was not going to get done. I had to slow down to move forward.

I refocused on my health, sat still, prayed and meditated every day until it became my number one priority! And then one day it happened. Voila—The *Book Thing* got done.

CATHY TRINH

LIVING SLOWLY TO TRANSFORM YOUR BODY: CANCER AND MORE

"You beat cancer by how you live, why you live and in the manner in which you live." —**Stuart Scott**

Early in 2018, I wound up in the emergency room at UCI during business hours with my sister for five hours with excruciating pain that shot up and down, alongside my neck and shoulders. Pain I had ignored for months. I had expansive and unexplained fullness in my throat and desperately needed it to be checked out.

I had a miscarriage weeks before finding out I had cancer. I knew there was something wrong with my body. I was feeling cold all the time, unable to eat and nauseous. Even though I was no longer pregnant, I was still feeling similar symptoms coupled with excruciating headaches, neck and shoulder pain and a sleuth of other medical ailments. I can't believe I allowed this pain in my throat area to go untreated for so many months.

A week later I found myself reclined on an exam table, scanned with an ultrasound and a big needle jabbed into my neck. I just stared at the ceiling, trying to remain calm despite the fear. I spent the previous evening Googling, "cancer in your neck," "biopsy needle," "lump in the neck," and "thyroid cancer death." The scan and biopsy revealed suspicious lumps on my thyroid gland.

By March 2018, I tested positive for cancer. My official diagnosis: metastatic papillary thyroid carcinoma (PTC). Cancer had spread into other regions of my neck. I was having trouble reconciling this information with the other facts of my life. I'm only 40, I thought to myself. I stopped smoking cigarettes years ago. I drink green juice and exercise. And the most important: *I can't be sick. I'm Noah's Mom.* Surgery was scheduled. Two back-to-back surgeries within months of each other. One to remove my thyroid and 14 lymph nodes and the second surgery to scrape cancer off my carotid artery, vocal nerve and the removal of ten more lymph nodes in my neck.

In April, I went under the knife for the first time. When I woke up, my throat was sore from the breathing tube, there was a drain in my neck, an IV in my arm, blood pressure cuffs on my legs and wires everywhere. The thyroid is a butterfly-shaped gland in the neck that powers your metabolism. It also plays a role in regulating body temperature and mood. It controls everything. After surgery, I was told I also needed radioactive iodine therapy, a type of radiation treatment also known as "RAI." However, radiation didn't happen immediately. Two months post-surgery, I was told a second surgery was necessary, as there was still more cancer that needed to be removed.

The second surgery was a success too. Cancer tissue was removed from my jugular vein, on my vocal nerve and behind my carotid artery. There was a chance of having vocal nerve paralysis, but he carefully maneuvered around the nerves and right jugular vein clamping it down in case it got nicked during the neck dissection. *"He didn't like bleeders!" he said.* The surgeon confirmed it was an extremely difficult surgery, but it worked very well. The next step was to receive radiation therapy to kill off micro-residue cancer cells that remained. I stayed in solitary confinement for a week and had to stay away from all living things. I managed very well in the hospital and throughout the treatments as everything was about having a positive mindset.

This was not the first time life had thrown me a curveball, so I tried to remain calm, telling myself I always find a way to work things out, or at least find an inch of silver lining. I am so thankful my cancer was treatable and that medication exists to replace what my vital gland once did. But let me tell you, life without a thyroid is not a piece of cake. I was perpetually tired and depressed, but also anxious. I feel cold when it is warm outside.

To prep for the radiation treatment, I was put on a low-iodine diet (no iodized salt, dairy, eggs, pizza, cheese or seafood) and given Thyrogen injections to rapidly raise my thyroid hormone levels to make the radiation effective at killing as many lingering cancer cells as possible. When I showed up in the Nuclear Medicine department in the basement of the hospital, the radiologist entered in a mask, lead apron and gloves to protect himself from the thing he wanted me to swallow. I signed the papers saying I would isolate myself from all living things for eight days. Scared and fascinated at the same time, I swallowed the pill and left the hospital with enough radiation to set off alarms at airports.

Now I see an endocrinologist every few months and I'm still struggling to find a good balance. I need more than a pill; I need energy, a healthy weight, happiness. My meds have been adjusted 2 times in an effort to achieve this and I'm trying to come to terms with the fact that I might never be symptom-free. That's why I bristle when I hear people say thyroid cancer is a "good" cancer – there's just no such thing.

On July 5th, 2020, I will celebrate one year in remission. 2018 and 2019 were the hardest years of my life but I got so much out of it. Being part of the "Big C club" is scary but it reminds me every day how amazing life is. If I could tell one person to check their neck today and they listened, then I've done my job. You can examine your own thyroid by feeling just above the collarbone on either side of the trachea with your fingertips—something I never did. Look out for any swelling or lumps.

I still remember the day I came to visit my cancer surgeon for the first time. The sun was shining on a beautiful Monday afternoon, my heart was still and I felt a sense of peace and calmness as I entered the examination room. It all happened in slow motion as if it was meant to happen exactly the way it did. I didn't even need to get a second opinion.

My doctor prepared me to go through three stages. The first stage is denial, then acceptance and finally the transformational phase. All three stages would be a gradual process and I wouldn't be able to accelerate the process even if I wanted to. My surgeon's wife was diagnosed with breast cancer several years prior and even his family needed to go through the same three stages. Even though he was a top ENT in Orange County he was not able to move his wife through these stages quickly to get to the transformational healing phase. During this transformative time, I learned several very powerful lessons about slowing down on my journey with Thyroid cancer. These lessons have now been anchored in my heart. A 4-inch scar on my neck is hard to miss, much like my tattoos, it will always serve a purpose to remind me of what has happened and to help me *slow down*.

Cancer isn't the life adventure I would have chosen from a list of possibilities or put on my bucket list, but it is the card that was dealt me in March 2018. And as it turned out, cancer had a lot to teach me about life. I believe in "*Miracles*". I also believe that having gone through my battle with cancer was also a miracle and a gift in itself so I can share my story to help others. *Life is a gift. Please cherish each Moment*

I will never forget the pain before and after I had surgery. When the pain meds wore off afterwards, I felt weak, had a pounding headache and my throat was sore. Frankly, I was quite scared. I didn't know what to expect upon coming to consciousness and how my life would change. I didn't know how life was going to be after surgery. Honestly, it didn't matter how my life would change, the only thing that was important was that I made it to the other side and had the opportunity to be *alive and enjoy life.*

Some of the lessons I learned and that are ingrained in me are:

- *Life is short; live slowly and embrace each Moment;*
- *Learn what is and is not controllable in life;*
- *Understand when to let go and when to take action;*
- *Know your personal sources of strength and hold them in your heart;*
- *Slow down, but increase motivation for change and take action.*

I became the best advocate for my health. I began to be conscious of what I put in my body such as food and medicine. I took care of my skin and my hair. I also practiced conscious living to make sure I kept toxic things out of my life, including people, places and things that were not conducive to my health. It's true that we become a product of our own environment. Therefore I made changes to be a better version of me. Now that I'm in remission, I use a more holistic approach to my life.

When you're faced with mortality and being in the midst of a storm, all you can do is continue to move forward. Life is purposeful, despite all the bumps in the road. It's been two years now since I was diagnosed and treated for cancer and I'm the happiest I've ever been in my life. With each challenge, we are presented with an opportunity to grow as a person. To choose to be passionate about improving yourself does not mean to say that you are not good enough for you are; it merely means you have a desire to expand into the greatest possible expression of yourself in this lifetime. We have to keep reinventing ourselves. Almost every minute, because the world can change in a heartbeat and there's no time for looking back. Sometimes the changes are forced upon us. Sometimes they happen by accident. We have to constantly come up with new ways to work on our growth.

"So we change, we adapt. We create new versions of ourselves. We make sure that this one is an improvement better than the last."—**Journal entry**, *November 20, 2018*

Every day we have the opportunity to evolve and transform our lives. Evolution happens for all of us, no matter how big or small, we evolve. I encourage everyone to continue to be the soul-shaper, free spirit, friend and lover that you were meant to be and go out to make an impact in this world. Live vivaciously and express your unbridled love for those who have affected you in positive ways. Transfer positive energy and move towards the light. Moments of time are priceless if we just take a Moment to breathe and appreciate them. The light of the Spirit has so many shades of love and compassion when we think and feel with our hearts.

DECLUTTERING IS GOOD FOR THE SOUL

"The glow of one warm thought is to me worth more than money." —**Thomas Jefferson**

Growing up in low income, blue collar immigrant home my parents kept everything, from broken toys, electronics, fabric, spare tile for home remodeling and clothes that have special meaning. I learned this trait and kept it for years and years. This character trait was useful in some sense, but it was detrimental in other areas. Not only was there physical clutter, but there was emotional, mental and spiritual clutter as well. I kept every piece of memorabilia from every relationship, place I've been, artwork my son drew, journal entry I wrote and important memory that meant something to me, whether good or bad.

In my coaching program, I was trained how to declutter – how to let go of the past and shed my old skin. I started to feel the freedom that was promised that I had not seen beneath all the years of self-abuse and mountain of stuff acquired. When I was in the relationship with my ex-husband, when he went into a manic episode, my son and I were the only family members that were able to help him pick up the pieces of his life when he went away to mental institutions or was locked up in jail for various lengths of time. This "picking up the pieces" caused us to lug around extra paperwork, trash bags with clothes, furniture and emotional baggage that didn't belong to us. Thank God this is no longer our lives. My son and I deserve peace and to be given the opportunity to live a less hectic life. Looking back, there is no blaming anyone for our lives – only curiosity and compassion.

For a long time, I was held back by needy, toxic people, unhealthy habits, old patterns of behavior and addictive substances. I know now that relationships kept me emotionally high, low and numb just like everything else. They were great distractions, but I would admit my picker was broken because I didn't have good examples to follow. I "used" relationships instead of being in them. In this way, I didn't have to look at my own issues. I was my best self when I was in fix it mode. As long as I had something or someone else to focus on that was more broken than me, it would keep me useful. *This, too, is a part of the journey."*

Broken and hurt people were really easy for me to find. They were hurt and needed to be rescued. *Who else would be the best person for the job?* I was codependent and abandoned myself. I was satisfied being in vacation-less, excuse filled, self-centered, too busy and ambitionless relationships.

My story wouldn't be complete if I didn't talk about two of the men that taught me the biggest lessons in my relationships in my life. My ex-husband and the man with the hearing impairment. These relationships led me to hit my worse spiritual and emotional bottoms. I really cared for these men tremendously, but I know today I couldn't save them. Looking back, I don't think I even knew what true love meant. I allowed things to happen in those relationships that I wouldn't even wish on my worst enemy. They were both bad at varying degrees, but it was hard for me to walk away despite all the pain. I stayed in the vicious cycle of thinking things would get better, he would change, if I only tried harder, or loved more. I was unable to walk away, but I knew there was a great life lesson in everything that was happening in my life. When you're stuck in a storm in the middle of the sea – you must weather the storm no matter what and if you come back safely to shore you will be stronger than you were before entering the waters. I knew there were reasons why I had to go through what I went through. The first main reason was having my son and the number two reason was to learn about unconditional love for myself. We must let go and let God in order to live a life beyond our wildest imaginations.

This long journey took me through deep self-reflection. I believe the root cause of my codependency stems from being the oldest of three daughters and accumulating strengths and weaknesses from my only two role models who were struggling emotionally themselves – my parents. It was only natural as I became an adult that I took on the role of caretaker, breadwinner, protector, rescuer, fixer, defender, "guardian angel", hero, liberator, salvager, deliverer and friend for those in need. These traits were poured into each relationship, but I also confused love with neediness.

I did my best to help my ex-husband stay on his meds to keep his mania under control. But I had to admit to complete defeat. I was truly powerless over his mental illness. It was an illusion on my part that I could fix him.

"I wanted to get inside his brain and turn the screws in the right direction, but that was not reality. I was becoming insane by thinking I was able to do this. My life had gotten so unmanageable and trying so desperately to rescue him caused me to become spiritually sick." —**Journal entry**, *October 21, 2017*

Self-sufficiency and the habit of acting as mother, nurse, breadwinner and caretaker took its toll on me. I finally realized I couldn't do it all myself. I did not have super-powers to fix someone else, if I wasn't even able to work on healing my own self. I was restored to sanity, by having faith in a Higher Power.

DEEPEN YOUR PRACTICE OF SLOWING DOWN

"We're all just walking each other home."
—Ram Dass

Every morning I wake up feeling so blessed and grateful. The gratitude of being alive and given another day to serve others is my gift to the world. I've been given a new lease on life because of the traumas I've able to escape. My heart beats, my lungs expand, my eyes blink, my feet move, my hands touch others, my mouth tastes, my nose smells and my body offers me life without asking for anything in return. If this is not the knowing that we are loved and are God's children, then I don't know how else to describe this. With the knowing of this deep love, I practice slowing down to embrace the gifts that I've been given. This practice includes mindful meditation practices and breathing exercises. It also includes listening to music, going outside into nature, putting the phone away, talking to God, calling Mom, telling people I love them and laughing until I pee my pants. I am essentially living life, having fun and doing worthwhile things while I still can with the time I have left. Most importantly I have slowed my life down enough to finish this book for all you highly fueled adrenaline junkies out there.

For years I self-harmed by putting chemicals into my body, working until sheer exhaustion, not eating nutritiously, stressed out over everything. Today, I practice all this goodness and am making amends to my body and spirit by incorporating what I do myself to teach my students and clients. I offer myself and these lessons in this book as a way of being of service and giving back what I was given throughout my life. I thank God, the Universe, Source Energy, Spirit and Gurus for all the lessons I've been given throughout my life. If this self-sabotaging, self-abandoning, adrenaline junkie can do it, you can slow down too.

"Self-love, self-respect, self-worth": There's a reason they all start with 'self.' You can't find them in anyone else but within you. Self-love is a journey. Self-love is an exponential force. It takes dedication, devotion and practice. Slowing down takes time and practice. Resolve to love yourself each and every day and watch your best self-blossom and your greatest life unfold! Imagine how you treat yourself on a daily basis as if you were another person, in a relationship with you.

Are you good to yourself? Is your mind kind to your body and soul?

I've discovered the practice of self-care on my journey and I am so happy I can share these practices with you. Today, I have a great daily ritual that supports me every day that I will share at the end of the book in my ***"7-day – Guide to Slow Living"*** that you can incorporate into your daily rituals too. One day at a time.

Self-care is the pathway to the greatest self-love.

CHAPTER TEN

THE "BIG CLEANSE"

"Moderate in order to taste the joys of life in abundance." —**Epicurus**

Many parts of this book were written during painful Moments in my life. Miscarriages, cancer treatment, breakups, job changes, death of loved ones and the painful withdrawal period in recovery were a few reasons I poured my heart onto paper and into this book. This was a period of deep spiritual cleansing for me.

This was a journey toward inward deep self-reflection that began for me many years ago. If you are like me and have picked up your pen, on and off again, *just keep going!* I know firsthand how hard it is to write anything positive when everything around you and within you is in complete disarray. The harsh reality for me was broken and I sought refuge in what felt most comfortable – social media, dysfunctional relationships, toxic behaviors, the list goes on and on. The cycle needed to *STOP!*

Making a decision to simplify and declutter my life allowed me to identify the toxic patterns and make better decisions. I called this phase in my life "*The Big Cleanse*". During this cleanse, I completely removed distractions. I had to identify what my biggest distractions were and refrain from acting out on them. I called these behaviors my baseline behaviors. Baseline is essentially the way of living that causes us to feel powerless and not in control of our lives. Sometimes these baselines are very destructive. For instance, I work remotely in a beautiful area surrounded by views of palm trees and greenery outside my window. I used to work in an enclosed office surrounded by cubicles and adrenaline fueled sales recruiters. My new life working remotely offers a new baseline way of living where it allows me to be more relaxed while I'm on the phone with my clients and recruiting candidates. My relationships with people who I speak with now have transformed into more deeper and present conversations versus sales driven tactics of working in a bull pen. Thus my baseline has been affected by the shift in dynamics in my office environment.

WHAT IS YOUR BASELINE?

"All you need is the plan, the road map, and the courage to press on to your destination." —**Earl Nightingale**

Your baseline can represent various ways of being. It also represents your core nature in any area of life. It is your decision how you decide to live with your true essence of who you are or how you show up in the world. The baseline can also represent how you see and act. It goes right to the essence of how you perceive your life. When you change your baseline living, you change your strengths.

Baseline behaviors, also known as *bottom line behaviors* (S.L.A.A. Program) are behaviors and activities that we must refrain from to experience physical, mental, emotional, sexual and spiritual wholeness. Acting out in these behaviors leads to a loss of self-control, self-identity and self-esteem. Self-abandonment and self-abuse sets in and we spiral down into emotional turmoil and dependency. Recovery begins when we admit that our lives have become unmanageable due to the loss of control in this area. *Baseline behaviors* are the low-vibrational behaviors that, if we choose to blindly continue engaging in, can lead us to keep hitting rock bottom. They are cycles of self-perpetuated, self-destructive, toxic behaviors.

Top line behaviors are behaviors that will be the bedrock in our healing journey. *"Top lines will serve to heal and support us in our recovery. "Over time these behaviors may change as more clarity comes and circumstances change."* (Reference: www.slaauk.org) It's important to stay on top of these top line behaviors to maintain emotional sobriety. They are conscious choices, actions, intentions and the way we choose to live life to fully actualize our best selves. This involves a lot of self-care practices, often incorporating tools of recovery programs and setting up daily self-care routines and rituals to sustain our emotional, physical, spiritual and mental health. You will find a number of top-line behaviors that you can use in my *"**7-Day Guide to Slow Living**"* at the end of this chapter.

For me, cleansing myself of *baseline behaviors* meant eliminating a lot of distractions and addictions. With some prior experience staying off social networks with my son, it was easy to make the choice to go social media (IG and Facebook) free for over a year. I also cleansed my life from the dating world for a whole year and remained off dating apps. I was the most addicted to dating apps. It is the land where broken people meet other broken people if you're not careful. The removal and abstinence from old destructive and self-sabotaging patterns allowed me to live a healthy and emotionally sober life, one day at a time.

I have been on social media since the age of 15 back in the AOL chatroom days. This affected my self-esteem, sense of self and gave me a warped view of my body. Comparing my life to strangers, friends and family members on my social media feed was not healthy for me. A revelation hit me that the larger the social media following, the smaller I felt. Comparing myself to others on social media made me feel utterly disappointed because I missed milestones and perceived "*deadlines*" in accomplishing life goals. It was also a huge distraction because it prevented me from actually focusing on projects and goals I did want to accomplish. Social media went away again this time for quite some time and life began to get quiet and slowed down again.

A part of this cleanse and decluttering process was journaling and capturing my daily "*Ah-ha*" Moments, challenges, heartbreaks, let downs, dysfunctional emotional behaviors and Momentary failures and set-backs every day. Daily reflection allowed me to clear and purge the pain when flashbacks from the past happened. Journaling captured times when I set fire to myself to keep another person warm. It also captured times when I caused self-harm and injury to my own heart.

Documenting Moments, pains, gains and losses is the only way to measure your progress and success in life. In my case, these maniacally written journal entries were written over the course of twenty years in over fifty journals in all colors, shapes and sizes. From notepads, voice memos, scrap paper and the back of calendars and inside of books. I wrote them to *never forget, but also as a way of letting go* just like the permanence in meanings of my tattoos.

I bought journals everywhere I went. At bookstores, grocery stores, gas stations and craft stores. Looking back on these journals, they indeed served a higher purpose. They helped me heal, grow and allowed me to experience miraculous breakthroughs, both personally and professionally. My life has been a *series of mini traumas* that allow me to be the woman I am today. My main purpose now is to help others heal on their journey. My hope is to move, touch, inspire and help others find peace in their lives and create the joyful life they deserve and love. I hope my roller coaster adventure allows you to free yourself from your imperfections.

Write or reflect as much as you can. Create a road map for your life. Self-reflection will allow you to shed the past and reveal the happiness you've been searching for. A diary is a map of your life, a chart of your growth, a record of your experience and a history of your past. Don't shut the door to your past, but use it as a navigational tool through life as you go on from here ever moving forward on the road to your happy destiny. I struggled with perfectionism, but I was far from perfect. I procrastinated for so long to find the perfect time to write this book and then I realized the perfect time was simply, now.

I was infatuated with Disney movies growing up with the inevitable happy ending. Disney movies were far from the truth, but I lived one helluva real-life story. Even though my life was riddled with sadness, there were so many incredible Moments. I've been able to document them as well. And I'm so glad I did.

My dream is to be up on a big stage with a mega microphone sharing my story with the world. To let people know that I've healed and want to make a difference in the world in a profound way. I survived war-time, childhood traumas, knee injury, eating disorder, chemical dependency, substance abuse, cancer and illness. I have also faced divorce, abortions, motherhood, manic entrepreneurship and majorly dysfunctional relationships.

I survived all of that and you will too!

THE H.O.L.Y. MOMENTS ©

"Acknowledging the good that you already have in your life is the foundation for all abundance." —**Eckhart Tolle, A New Earth:** Awakening to Your Life's Purpose

Early on in the book, I introduced a concept called ***H.O.L.Y. Moments*** ©. I developed this belief in 2019 as a new way of spiritual living and thinking as there have been so many coincidences, synchronicities and spiritual alignments that have happened in my life that I can only describe as ***a holy Moment***. Not as in a religious Moment, but as special Moments. The present Moment. The present day. These times are Moments that we can create at any given minute if we allow ourselves to bring ourselves to the highest level of awareness of our surroundings. This includes breathing, eating, thinking, slowing down, working, writing, cleaning, decluttering, manifesting, living, smiling, feeling, enjoying, etc. The list can go on and on! We can obtain these special Moments especially while we are in the stillness and quiet of our lives. These are miraculous gifts captured when we pay attention to them.

This concept or new way of spiritual living will to allow you to experience the miracles in your life as you build awareness in the four types of ***H.O.L.Y. Moments* ©.** These four types of Moments are defined as ***H**olistic,* ***O**rganic,* ***L**ittl*e, and ***Y**earned* Moments in our lives. If you are able to recognize the kind of Moment you have, you will allow you to be able to appreciate these Moments for what they are as you journey through your life.

These Moments may offer you a breakthrough or insights into your life as you are experiencing them. I have experienced many ***H.O.L.Y. Moments*** © on my journey and have embraced the miracles from these Moments. Now I can apply what I've experienced as well as relate to these Moments in my life. I am very excited to share a few of my special ***H.O.L.Y. Moments*** © stories with you in hopes that you will take the time to slow down and appreciate your life. Create happiness, joy, and love every day from this point forward!

Lastly, I would highly suggest that you start a personal journal to jot down every ***H.O.L.Y. Moment***© that you mindfully experience throughout your day. Journaling helps you meet your goals and will improve the quality of your life. It can help you clear your head, connect essential thoughts, feelings and behaviors that affect your wellbeing as well as mental health. This is a repeated paragraph from the beginning of my book, however I feel it is very important and relevant to help you on your journey with identifying your special ***H.O.L.Y. Moment* ©.**

Write down your favorite "slowing down" H.O.L.Y. Moment and what you are committed to practicing. Keep a record of your experiences and results. It is a great way to self-reflect to see what's working or not working in your life. This journal will be especially helpful for the **Seven (7) Day *"Guide to Slow Living"*** located at the end of this chapter. Enjoy each Moment and the pace of your daily journey as you get to experience it, as I have done on mine.

Feel free to email as you read through these my examples if you're having one of the following ***H.O.L.Y. Moments*©**. I would love to hear from you: Cathy@CathyTrinh.com

What is a H.O.L.Y. Moment ©?

H. Holistic Moments
O. Organic Moments
L. Little Important Moments
Y. Yearned Moments

The Present.
The Now.
This is it.

(H.O.L.Y) HOLISTIC MOMENTS©

"A wise man ought to realize that health is his most valuable possession." —**Hippocrates**

Holistic [hō'listik]
ADJECTIVE
Parts of something as intimately interconnected and explicable only by reference to the whole. Treatment of the whole person.
Synonyms: *comprehensive, integrated, entire, full, universe, total*

What allows you to experience a ***H.O.L.Y. (Holistic) Moment***? There is not one person in this world that can feel and live this Moment better than you. We always strive to be better, do better, but we still fear making a change. Living in peace and harmony can holistically heal our minds, body and soul. Daily we need to make a conscious effort to have a better life.

I've personally experienced these Holistic Moments that were all a part of my gradual spiritual awakening process. We all move forward or slip backward, but in retrospect, I can see the change for the better between my old and new self. I will continue to see a better new person with these methods. Nothing has done more to move me forward than carrying the message of hope and recovery to those who are still suffering, unable to take care of themselves.

I encourage each one of you to live a natural, holistic lifestyle. Take care of yourself by nurturing your whole being, restore your mind, body and spirit to a balanced state with universal energy. Live by your own rules and truths – work towards being the best version of yourself and be flexible in embracing growth and change. Living holistically and experiencing holistic Moments in your life is living in a way that is natural to you and the world within which you live. Use natural therapies that benefit you physically, emotionally, spiritually, socially and mentally.

You can live a holistic experience by keeping your mind and body active, practicing yoga and meditation and eating organic foods often. You can experience physical, emotional, mental and spiritual Holistic Moments in life. Physical Holistic Moments occur when you listen to your body. Our bodies send us messages of imbalance at some level. You can remedy the imbalance in your body by using massage, physiotherapy, chiropractic care, acupuncture, or doing yoga and meditation. There are traditional and natural therapies you can use alongside modern medicines. Our bodies are beautiful and will let us know when something is not right.

My mistake growing up was I used to go to the doctor for prescription pills in hopes of fixing a symptom. A tablet for when my body was in pain. A tablet when my mind filled with hopelessness. A tablet when my heart was broken to numb the sadness. After a long road of suffering and addiction, I made a conscious decision to take the holistic route to treat the cause of my health issue rather than use a pill to solve all the brokenness.

During my cancer treatments, I paused amid all the chaos and created a holistic lifestyle by using a wholefood plant-based diet. All my life, I ate processed meats and dairy products. Eating too much dairy had an adverse effect on bowel movements and intestines. I went to a gastroenterologist and was diagnosed with GERD (Gastroesophageal Reflux Disease), which is a chronic digestive disease where the liquid content of the stomach refluxes into the esophagus. It can be relieved through diet and lifestyle changes. (Reference: www.webmd.com). I was advised by the physician to not eat certain foods that cause reflux, such as spices and milk products that had high levels of acid or lactose.

I will never know why I got cancer, but I do know that prescription pills and amphetamine drug changed the way I think and the way body was affected by the drugs. I remember my rapid heartbeats causing an alarming heart condition, sweaty palms, blotchy skin, brittle hair, erratic thinking, constant depression and anxiety.

Keeping a positive frame of mind is so important. Letting go of negative energy that does not serve you or add value to your life are Holistic Moments that will keep you balanced on an emotional level. I was afflicted with depression, stress and anxiety from all my drug abuse, alcoholism and addiction my entire life. I was in so much pain from the emotional roller coasters and the energy they took that I didn't want to wake up and live anymore. Every day I felt like I was surviving to take care of my son, pay the bills and get by. Every day hurt, stuck in the vicious cycle of addiction. Eventually, I overcame the turmoil by practicing holistic care by using the following remedies.

On a ***mental level,*** I let go of limiting beliefs, perceptions, judgments and other people's opinions of me. I believe that I am my own person and am unique.

On a ***spiritual level,*** I spent time in nature and found a deeper connection with myself. I spent time looking at the stars, watched sunsets and continued to dream and embrace what I believed. I kept my soul happy. I practiced the gift of being of service, performing random acts of kindness, smiling at strangers, decluttering my space and letting go of things that no longer served my present-day life.

I have tried to incorporate a holistic lifestyle since I was young, but I kept losing my way during all the trials and trauma of addiction. At some point in my life, I suffered body and lower back pain, stressed out about life and allowed negative energy around me to take over my life. I was unmotivated and uninspired to seize the day. I felt hopeless. When I made a conscious decision to create a routine to eat more natural foods, practice yoga and balance my mind with Morning Prayer and meditation, my life began to change. I let go of negative energy around me and blocked negative thoughts about the way people thought of me. I began to feel free and motivated.

I lost weight; my back and knee pain went away. I'm in the best shape of my life, mind, body and soul. Consistency is key to living a happy life. You can make wise choices on who you keep in your life, what you put in your body and places you choose to go.

When you change your life and intentionally live a holistic lifestyle, you are choosing to heal your mind and body naturally. You begin to observe your life in its entirety as a whole. You view spiritual, mental and emotional sickness in the big picture. You become more prepared and equipped for life's challenges rather than running to a drink, drug, relationship or life's problem. You choose to heal through the magical healing wonders of the universe.

Here are a few ways to reach higher, vibrational, relaxed and holistic Moments in your life.

- ***Slow down and live in the Moment—practice*** mindfulness. Living in the present is an essential way of having a holistic lifestyle.
- ***Recognize and respect your body as a temple.*** Tap into the hidden powers of your body and use it towards your advantage. Practice meditation. It helps you relax and feel connected to the earth. We are all connected.
- ***Practice a healthy lifestyle & clean eating.*** Being free from drugs, alcohol and unhealthy habits will keep your mind and body healthy. Try home-cooked meals. It will keep you happier since you're able to control what you're eating and putting in your meals. Eat organic, fresh fruits and vegetables and lean meats.
- ***Encourage yourself and others to focus on positive relationships.*** Negative energy, being upset in life or stressed will keep you stuck and won't allow you to have space to put positive things in your life.
- ***Value your time, don't overcommit, overdo and push yourself to the limit.*** Being selfish with time is a healthy way of living. Don't rush and try to maximize your time.
- ***Allow yourself to grow.*** You will go through periods of life-changing events. Modify your character traits and life one step at a time. Take baby steps if you need to and take the time to grow and live a holistic lifestyle. Nurture yourself with love and care.
- ***Love yourself.*** Sometimes you are dealt a bad hand and at other times you've hit the lottery. That's life. Don't feel bad when you reach a low point. We all hit weak points in our lives. Keep going. Keep growing. Through the pain, there is always a silver lining in each dark Moment.
- ***Be respectful to others and love your neighbors.*** You never know what battles someone is going through in life during each season of their lives. Your kind words might be the push that is needed to stop them from hurting.
- ***Connect with others that are on similar paths.*** It will be easier to live holistically by being around people who are on the same page and chosen path. Connecting with others who are on a similar journey will improve your way to a better life.

- ***Be aware.*** The ability to be prepared for what life throws at you and being able to observe your surroundings is a way to live holistically.
- ***Meditation.*** The art of meditation can improve your life by setting aside time to sit, relax and focus on your breathing. It's an effective method for dealing with stress and allows you to make more sound decisions.
- ***Stay active.*** Keep your body always vibrant and get fresh air by going for a swim, walk, jog or hike. Incorporating exercise into your daily life will allow you to feel great about yourself.

When we change our energy and mindset, we improve our life. Our mindset determines which road we travel on. Our path is either paved with scarcity or filled with abundance. Those who choose to walk along the path of abundance experience a different life with love, freedom, happiness, joy, gratitude, learning and endless possibilities. Those who live in a scarcity mindset will feel they never have enough, both emotionally and physically, even if they are surrounded by excess that others don't have. Opt to live life to the fullest, exuding happiness, generosity by nature, creativity and inspiration. Take full advantage of being alive by having a grateful heart and enjoy the opportunities that do come your way.

My loving affirmation:

"Today, I will love and treat my body with love and care. I am making living amends to my body and taking care of it with regular exercise, meditation and relaxation. This helps me feel balanced, energized and emotionally stable. The best feeling is when I feel healthy, fit and happy."

(H.O.L.Y.) ORGANIC MOMENTS©

"People fall in love in mysterious ways. Maybe it's all part of a plan." —**Ed Shereen**

Organic [ôr'ganik]
ADJECTIVE
Elements that fit together harmoniously as parts of a whole. Living matter. Produced without artificial agents.
Synonyms: *living, live, animate, natural, harmonious, biotic*

I've fallen in love a few times in my life. Those relationships were the best relationships and they happened naturally and organically. They flowed into the state of love from the first time we met. Live and love organically. With all the relationship mishaps throughout my life, it was a common theme for me to believe that being single meant that something was missing in my life. I obsessively looked for what I considered a missing piece of myself. In these inorganic Moments, I continued to search for the concept of what love was; however, my lack of self-worth prevented the natural organic flow of relating to a man.

I was able to open myself up to the possibility of love again once I honed in on becoming more authentic and allowing love to develop organically by using the concept of the **O** in *H.**O**.L.Y Moments.*

In these *Organic Moments,* I used the visual of gardening as a template to follow when it came to cultivating loving and organic partnerships. To have this love, it takes time to nurture a budding relationship. Just like when you plant a seed, it takes time and gentle care to assist in the blossoming process. It's the same when it comes to relationships. Every relationship is different and the foundation you need to build on is the relationship you have with yourself, as described in my *"Relationship quadrant"* of my coaching program. It's essential to keep balance and set positive goals to deepen your relationship with others, but it is equally important to maintain a healthy relationship with yourself. The natural unfolding of the process determines the quality of your life. Anything that doesn't allow the natural unfolding of love organically will not survive its full potential.

Each potential relationship should be nurtured and not be related to preconceived concepts with a time frame for development. Adopting this concept allows the energy and love to flow more efficiently and it creates a path of least resistance to develop naturally and organically.

One time, I met a man through an online connection and had the chance to experience this natural and organic type of relationship. I didn't put pressure on both of us to use this organic process. We were relaxed and had a lot of fun getting to know each other. My mindset was that if I didn't have this person as a new partner, I would potentially gain a new friend. I allowed each experience and encounter to unfold naturally and reveal its unique treasure. I learned in this relationship that developing an organic, deeper bond happened through creating authentic friendships.

Although we only knew each other for a short time, we had many ***Organic H.O.L.Y. Moments.*** From the first time we met each other, our first kiss, the sweet mornings together, to being in the kitchen and cooking together – they all felt organic. We both had a genuine concern for each other that led to a comfort zone that ended up being the catalyst for the feeling of safety, love and orgasmic bliss. I felt safe being with him and this level of security that we both shared determined the depth of our vulnerability with one another. The more we opened up, the more pleasure we experienced during the highest vibration with one another during times of intimacy.

I stepped outside of my comfort zone of using men as a crutch and embraced this lover. I allowed faith in the process to manifest love and present itself in whatever way I did. And as luck would have it, we enjoyed the tenderness and love we found with one another. Unfortunately, as organically as it came – organically it went – however this time around with the knowledge I've gained from my program and what I know today about relationships, I will no longer control or force the outcome of a relationship that is not meant for me. I'm able to walk away with dignity and grace. Although my hope was for a long term relationship, we were spiritually misaligned and had differences in values. With the support of my program, I was able to cut the losses sooner, so that I could continue my search for a long-term companion and partner to walk with on my journey. This chapter in my love life shall be continued…

Here are several ways to create a blissful connection and manifest "***Organic H.O.L.Y. Moments***" to develop organic relationships:

- ***Release the past and come from a place of clarity and nothingness.*** Release the pressure of needing something to develop.
- ***Organically connect with others.*** Eliminating the checklist and accepting your potential partner, friend or loved ones without any judgment allows you to feel more comfortable with exposing deeper aspects of yourself. You will be able to see others beneath the societal mask and possibility for compatibility, whether at dating, work, school or at home.
- ***Release the need and pressure for something to develop.*** Relaxing and socially interacting will expand each relationship through new experiences which will build a stronger bond than what you see on the surface.
- ***Allow attraction to develop naturally.*** There needs to be a strong foundation built on respect, trust and integrity. Don't get caught up on the physical attributes. You will organically develop a framework for the physical bond as it forms over time.

Many times in the past, I pushed away from the love I "*needed*" because it didn't match the love I "*wanted*." These expectations I had with men blocked me from experiences that were able to open me up to a more profound, expansive love. Today, I know that this expansive love I have desired all my life will organically come once I meet someone who values the same things in life and the connection and bond will happen naturally.

(H.O.L.Y.) LITTLE MOMENTS©

"Enjoy the little things, for one day you may look back and realize they were the big things." —**Robert Breault**

Little ['lidl]
ADJECTIVE
Small in size, special small Moments, the simplicity of small and little Moments in life that add up to an entire journey. The most precious things often come in small, simple, little packages. The purest Moments are often quiet and little.
Synonyms: *small-scale, modest, minimal, simple, precious, quiet Moments*

The little things in life are those that make us the happiest. They are the special Moments in life that give us the greatest amount of happiness. They come in the simplest forms and sometimes come unexpectedly. They are the special, sacred, small Moments of simplicity in life that add up to an entire journey. They can be small Moments of joy, peace, quiet pleasures, or little Moments of synchronicities, signs and realizations.

These ***Little H.O.L.Y. Moments*** could change your life and leave a profound lasting impact. Sometimes they are the little things we barely notice that happened to us that we may not have planned as opposed to big things that we expect. People naturally feel excited during significant life events such as getting married, first homes, newborn babies, job promotions or even a considerable holiday and so on. But in between those big Moments are the small Moments that point us in the right direction and teach us great lessons of life.

It's the little things in life that I pay close attention to nowadays. There have been many such small and unnoticeable occurrences in my life that I've allowed slip past me overlooking them as coincidences. But I later realized nothing is a coincidence. I've received many calls from old friends or family members who dialed my number within minutes of me thinking of them. It's like we are connected in thoughts and feelings! Magical Moments where I have said something and within seconds the radio or TV emits the same frequency or wavelength I'm on, channeling the message through the device in which I am watching or listening to.

There were games I've played with myself to see if something is going to happen or if I am able to receive a gift of some sort – and suddenly, they all happened as I declared. Are these coincidences or were they meant to happen? When you can tune in, you will awaken to realize that you're the one that is playing the game of life with a greater Source of consciousness and guardian guiding and orchestrating, gifting you many clues and signs along the way on the treasure hunt of life. As you become more aware of your actions and behaviors, your life gets better. These are some of the spiritual gifts I have received in life when I am hyper aware of my surroundings. Once I made this discovery, I never turned a blind eye again, no matter how small and insignificant it feels. There is a purpose for everything that happens in your life.

A few years ago, I experienced a ***Little H.O.L.Y. Moment*** situation that yielded financial success – a win for our firm and myself. This situation only happened because I was present and awake spiritually. This situation occurred while I was walking into the Main Place Mall in Santa Ana and it presented a massive win for our search firm within eight months. As I was walking into the mall, on a beautiful business day in my non-business attire to return something, I went into my wallet to pull out a receipt and a dime flew out of my purse, hit the floor and rolled behind me. *"It's only a dime!"* I told myself and continued walking towards the entrance of the mall. A few seconds later, a man picked up the dime and walked swiftly towards me to hand me my money.

It turned out this man, walking to the mall with his CFO for lunch, was someone I knew through a mutual recruiter friend who worked for a $700 million privately owned healthcare company. Shortly after lunch, we connected on Linkedin. One swift conversation after the next, I was in a client visit doing an intake order for several accounting searches they had open. Within several weeks, we placed a few consultants – accumulating billings of over $80,000 for our recruiting services for consultants and a temp-to-hire conversion. Not only did this happen, but this little Moment also created several strong life-long friendships and business partnerships. I've shared this story and my dear and now lifelong friend & client Mark over the years calling it our special "***Dime Story***", an *"L" Moment.*

This experience is proof that little things in life can result in massive results in the end if we are present and aware of what is going on in our lives at all times. I have practiced this concept in all my affairs with a heightened level of importance in everything I do, no matter how small.

Here are some simple, little things in daily life that can bring you true happiness:

- *Take an extra-long bath or shower when you have free time.*
- *Call a friend, family member or loved one and check in on them.*
- *Be present with your children and enjoy each Moment you can.*
- *Smile at strangers and be kind to one another.*
- *Enjoy the little things at home, at work and play.*
- *Keep track of small things.*
- *Thank someone for small things.*
- *Compliment someone for small things.*
- *Appreciate yourself for the small things.*
- *Live in the Moment and appreciate the little things in life.*

Enjoy the little things in life because one day you'll look back and realize they were actually significant milestones in life. Having the ability to appreciate the small things in life can upgrade your life in a magnificent way. There is a reason to celebrate the small things and be grateful everyday no matter how small. *Gratitude is a powerful attitude* that will continue to attract that same energy of graciousness and high vibration of love and awareness into all aspects of your life.

(H.O.L.Y.) YEARNED MOMENTS©

"My favorite things in life don't cost any money. It's really clear that the most precious resource we all have is time." —**Steve Jobs**

Yearn [yərn]
VERB
Have an intense feeling of longing for something.
Synonyms: *long, crave, desire, want, wish, hunger, thirst*

In the midst of an emotional storm from a painful breakup, I received a cancer diagnosis that changed my life and perspective. All of a sudden I felt scared, angry, sad, discouraged and heartbroken all at once. The next several months felt like forever. Time slowed down and the Moment of peace I yearned for felt like they were never going to arrive. I felt like I should have been further along in life. I kept dreaming of a world I thought I was never going to see.

And then one day it happened for me. I woke up and I was in a place where everything simply felt right. A place I'd yearned to arrive at all my life. No sweaty palms, a steady heartbeat, no racing thoughts or pressured speech. A place where my heart was calm and my soul was lit brighter than ever before. My thoughts were positive and my vision was clear. I was at peace. At peace with where I'd been. At peace with what I'd been through and at peace with where I'm headed now.

As I poured every ounce of my heart and experience into this book, I learned so many lessons. I kept pushing forward and never stopped, even when I was in the hospital room before surgery. Nothing was going to stop me. I made it happen. I finished the book and that Moment I *yearned* for all my life, happened.

AFFIRMATIONS FOR GROWTH:

- ❖ I AM whole, even as I grow.
- ❖ I AM more than any negative thoughts of insecurity, shame, or separation.

- I AM willing to deepen my awareness and expand my perception to embrace a more whole, loving view of myself as I live in the world.
- I AM more than the sum of my parts and I am part of something greater.

AFFIRMATIONS FOR SLOWING DOWN:

- I AM enjoying the people who are in my life, right now.
- I AM enjoying the journey and making the conscious choice to slow down.
- I AM making time to observe life and taking the time to simply be.
- I AM scheduling life in a way where I can have some rest and live comfortably in peace
- I AM taking the time to simply inhale and exhale.
- I AM centered and quiet and exactly where I am supposed to be.
- I AM unwinding, steady and aware.
- I AM breaking the habit of "busy" and acquainting myself with the world under my feet.

I know as long I follow any path with the intention of moving forward, learning and growing, my life will just come together as the Universe intended. There were Moments I was disconnected from my true Self and higher power. My inner voice, the inner critic in me was never satisfied. It was so loud that it dominated my landscape of thoughts. I lost my way. However meaningful I thought my life was, there was always another place I longed to be. I was born with high intuition, insight and consciously aware, yet I was not always honing my gifts or living aligned with my Soul purpose and higher Self.

I yearned to be loved, to feel safe and have a home.

CATHY TRINH

SLOWING DOWN TO THE SYMPHONY OF LIFE

"The effect you have on others is the most valuable currency there is." —**Jim Carrey**

The Importance of *Slowing Down* in the COVID-19 "Coronavirus" Era:

Life is a collection of gifts and your past has brought you to this point in time. You are reading this because you value your personal growth, inspired to unleash your full potential and have a desire to realize your destiny. This is the process of life. Nothing is certain other than the knowledge you acquire on your journey that leads to your soul's growth.

In late 2019, the world got hit by a novel and dangerous pandemic, known as the COVID-19 or "Coronavirus" killing thousands worldwide with continuously rising numbers and no vaccine in sight. Corona in Latin means "crown", referring to the crown-like halo on the virus when looked at through a microscope. It is a ruthless virus – nothing the modern world has ever faced with no effective vaccination as of yet. We are told that it is able to survive for up to twenty three hours outside of the human body. Since it is airborne, any surfaces it lands on if touched could spread the infection too. It is also is asymptomatic within a host for two weeks or more and documented at even 40 plus days, all the while spreading to many others, causing a rampant global pandemic.

As of April 4, 2020, COVID-19 has taken the lives of thousands and thousands of people, which included elders worldwide and those with compromised immune systems, as well as the young and healthy. It has crept into the younger age brackets, especially taking the lives of courageous doctors and nurses who work directly with infected patients. COVID-19 hit China, Iraq and Italy especially hard and then spread to all other countries, including the United States.

By mid-March, 2020, an Executive Order was placed in the United States for all businesses to cease working for fourteen days within my city and throughout the entire nation. It then extended to an extra month with no approximate date as to when the epidemic will cease. Schools were closed initially for two then, shut down for the remainder of the school year. Our children were officially all "home-schooled." We don't know when they will reopen. Life as we knew it had completely changed.

We now have national laws to self-quarantine, "shelter-in-place" and "social distance" for indefinite months with the conditions getting worse and worse as infections and deaths keep rising. Social distancing and quarantined sites include all the Alano clubs offering support for those in recovery from drug and alcohol addiction, restaurants, gyms, stores and any public place of gatherings of any size including parks and any place outside in groups. This pandemic is an incredibly scary and troubling time.

During quarantine, I utilized Zoom to participate in support group meetings with up to hundreds of other addicts and alcoholics across the nation sharing the message of experience, strength and hope to support each another. I love how our community has coming together to help each other. The topic of discussion that came up one morning is, *"Why do we keep coming back*?" For me I keep coming back to recovery programs because of the proof that the programs work. The global connection and a strong sense of community among one another, no matter our walks of life, has been more reliable than ever. Especially during these times of crisis, when in-person services are not available, many of us come together for love, compassion, empathy and support in online meetings. These tumultuous times remind me of 9-11. September 11th was also a very fragile time for all of us in our country. Especially for those families surviving the loss of their loved ones, with over 2,977 innocent lives lost.

September 11th, 2001 was a time I will never forget. I was going through a very challenging time in my personal and professional life. Before the second plane crashed into the next tower, I was escorted out of the office I was working at. I was fired because I was under the influence of drugs and made inappropriate conspiracy statements to a co-worker sitting in the cubicle next to me on the state of our nation. This was before more modernized social media rants and Facebook capabilities. I spoke my mind and said a few things that offended people I worked with at the office. For many years, I kept that bottled up inside for fear that others would judge me for the mental and spiritual state I was in during that time in my life. Angry. Unstable. Unsound. Incoherent. For years and years, I kept this incident to myself for fear that if you knew me and who I was, "*You would not like me.*"

I no longer feel that statement holds the truth. I am loveable, whole and complete today. Today, I accept all of my flaws and who I am as a person. As I take a Moment to reflect on the years that followed that incident of losing my job during a horrific act of violence against America, I know I had to go through that experience to become a brave person to talk about this today. All the years of low self-esteem and insecurity I endured after the incident has made me a reliable person because of the lessons I've learned. Especially during the COVID-19 outbreak and recession that we are all going through as a community worldwide, it is taking great strength in me to remain calm and finish this book project to speak my truths during this time.

Everyone is going through something at work, at school, at home, in the air, on land and at sea. It's so important to stay connected to people as much as we can today in society as a whole. This pandemic has forced everyone to slow down in life and reflect on what is essential, such as our collective health, our families, our lives and all the lives of others interconnected to us globally. We are all asked to physically, mentally and spiritually slow down as we all have to bunker in place and truly reprogram ourselves and be introspective in healing ways. This pandemic reveals that to truly heal as a world, we need to care about one another in the same way we care about our health because we all co-exist in a very intricate web of existence.

As I continue to follow the news locally, nationally and globally, receiving information from the Orange County Health Agency with updated messages from our school superintendent and the media, it gives me such an unsettling feeling. I am sure everyone is going through this same internal panic and worry. I pray that we all continue to be as healthy as possible and together brave the COVID-19 storm together. I intend to share my message of hope while the world is appearing to be crumbling down, forcing us to slow down, go within and come together to heal the earth and society. Sharing my message of connectedness and spiritual healing is so relevant and necessary during this time.

COVID-19 will come and go. I am reminded how fear can control our lives. Fear in our hearts, minds and life as we know it. From our local community, our financial institution, to our government, I will never forget how easy it is for them to take full control of our lives. Access to every sporting event, classroom, restaurant table, support gathering, church pew and even food supply is under the control of our government. We are asked not to leave our own homes for our safety and the safety of others.

During this time, the news flashes with an overwhelming sense of fear in our society, communities, locally and worldwide. On the news, our California Governor, Gavin Newsom, sent out a sobering but responsible message. Students, teachers and parents have been warned not to expect schools to be back in session within a few weeks, that they will not reopen until after summer break in efforts to increase social distancing, especially among vulnerable populations. During this time, schools and colleges across the state have been hit by a wave of closures and cancellations of work to prevent the spread of the Coronavirus. The new normal – children are being homeschooled by parents who are desperately trying to continue working from home to provide income and pay basic needs. Those less fortunate have been laid off and do not have income at all to support the families. A reported 3.3 million people filed for unemployment in one week. The working class is waiting with worry to receive the $1,200 stimulus check that the government has promised to issue.

There is also emergency legislation proposed to provide billions in funding to help fight COVID-19. This money is going to provide more hospital beds and medical equipment to help hospitals deal with the coming surge and protect those who are most at risk. Our medical doctors, nurses and medical staff are not well-equipped with PPE (Personal Protective Equipment) such as face masks, gowns and gloves in preparation for the surge of patients who have COVID-19. New York City has been struck the hardest due to population density and not heeding the warnings of the upcoming crisis. Many doctors and nurses are becoming infected and some regretfully have passed away as well. Hospital beds, ventilators and supplies are all in short supply. Hospital staff are struggling to treat the sheer amount of infected patients as well.

As the spread of COVID-19 is surging around the globe, humankind is being brought closer together than at any other time in our nation's history.

From all this pain and suffering, there is always a lesson to be learned. *An awakening of sorts.* At the time of writing this chapter, it has only been a month, but this virus has already made a major impact on humanity. As the world endures heartbreaking losses, these tragedies break down cultural barriers in a mutual effort to defend the human race and protect the most vulnerable. When life hangs on a thread of human survival, *once divisive issues,* such as skin color, politics and religious beliefs, take a backseat. The urgency of the situation forces us as a culture and world to reprioritize war and seek peaceful healing as a global world. I've experienced this in my own life. Spending time with my son, slowing down, getting things around my house settled and making sure things within my own home are right and balanced have been a top priority, whereas they were lower on my daily task list before this.

Our world has helped us understand that good cannot come from evil. Good can, however, occur in response to evil and suffering. Human greed, how we mistreat and abuse one another, is a powerful evil. Yet compassion can grow among very different peoples. From all the wars in the world, such as the Vietnam War, the Jewish Holocaust and the days following the great trauma of 9-11, to what is happening today – in all of these extremely painful experiences, human lives were lost. Humanity has felt extreme pain, numbness, hatred and anger. The horrific loss of life in New York City, the lives lost at the Pentagon and the innocent who died aboard United Airlines Flight 93 rocked the consciousness of America and throughout the world. All of these events have forced us all to go into survival and revival mode.

With the COVID-19 pandemic worldwide, people panicked and began buying and fear hoarding everything at the grocery stores, especially toilet paper. There were videos of people physically fighting and hurting each other to stock up. Some parents couldn't find milk and formula for their infants and children. There were great anti-Asian racist sentiments as the Coronavirus was called "*The Chinese Virus*" even by our current President Trump himself, which caused great confusion and division among the American people. Some Asians around the world were being violently attacked with ignorant racial slurs yelled at them. There is ignorance and separation, but humankind has also united with one mission to fight against this terrible disease globally.

This pandemic has come close to apocalyptic scenes in a horror movie that we are all waiting to end. Yet, there is great compassion growing from the suffering as well. We see communities and people speaking up and taking actions to protect the elders and disabled, various communities offering to grocery shop or cook for homebound elders. Stores have opened special designated hours just for seniors and disabled people to shop without the craziness of crowds. Schools continue to provide free breakfast and lunches for children and the disabled. Nursing mothers who have excess milk are connecting online to donate their milk to other infants whose mothers cannot produce milk but cannot find formula.

Organizations and therapists are offering community support virtually online. Communities continue the political narrative and long-overdue fight for HealthCare 4 All as we are also in the middle of the election season for 2020 Presidential campaigns. The issue of Universal Healthcare and prioritizing human life over profit will become central, driven by great love and compassion for all of humanity, but also realizing how critical it is for the survival of us all inter-connectedly. The *Awakening* of the COVID-19 pandemic has helped us all come together and rally for all human life and hopefully respect nature and the Earth going forward.

During this time, we are rallying as a global community to support one another. Differences in background, belief and lifestyle fade. We work together to support the families who suffer a loss. I now live as a conscious being with my only mission to help my community in hopes of passing the torch for future generations to come. Let's pray together and rise above the "large and small stuff" and strengthen the cords that bind us together to grow stronger as individual people and as a collective humanity. This pandemic has brought people together from all walks of life, around the world offering help to one another more than ever before. This is more than a global pandemic, but more a spiritual or Universal cleansing. It served as a hard reset for everyone globally. To help shift our perspectives to what is most important in life such as family, health, love and compassion for one another.

There is a silver lining to the chaos. There is a greater lesson to the suffering.

From nothing, we can create anything. Restructuring of communities and governments if need be. Restructuring and redefining our own lives, homes and ourselves. The pandemic is creating more values within families, who now care less about material things, and who care more about the environment and appreciate life in general. Many of us will have the opportunity in the coming weeks and months to do this. During this time, I am taking a look at the world around me and also within myself. I spend time looking out the window to gaze at the beautiful palm trees and greenery that surround the front entrance of my apartment home. Even though I can't visually see other parts of the Earth with my naked eye, I see it through my mind's eye. I see by using my five senses and memories of my travels throughout the world to parts of Europe with my girlfriends, Asia visiting long-distance family and Brazil during the World Cup soccer games. A mind is a powerful tool of connection when we allow it to be.

The world is vast and beautiful. There's still so much to see and explore and I hope you get an opportunity to take the time to go and soak it all in once this pandemic is contained and healing is restored on Earth all over the world. For now, as we hunker down and "shelter-in," make sure you take a few moments to reflect on everything you have to be grateful for. While you're not as busy as usual, pick up your phone and make a meaningful phone call. Call those you love, especially the elderly, the younger children in your life that don't understand what's going on, the person you have been thinking about but haven't reached out to and the ones you think might be struggling and needing support most. During this critical time of "staying in", I am able to enjoy the simpler things in life such as reading, napping, writing, board games, laughter, storytelling, going for walks, playing, expressing through arts and crafts, learning something new and quiet hikes with my loved ones.

Sometimes in life, things happen that aren't according to plan and you make the most of it. Every season has a reason and so does this critical time in our collective lives. Our ability to be flexible and open-minded during these moments of our experiences of discomfort and dis-ease can determine so much. My hope for everyone is that you are able to stay calm, level headed, connected within, no matter whatever is happening, and make the most of what is going on in life through this period of immense slowing down. Life is asking us to slow down, truly without an option this time, and we must listen to all heal.

Amid this Coronavirus madness, I am incredibly grateful for the privilege of continuing to take this journey of deep self-reflection and produce a book that will embody my life's work to help inspire, uplift and possibly heal those who are suffering. I am grateful to be fully immersed in supporting others, steer them away from toxic addictions and offer solutions that can help people cope with all the anxiety, stress and craziness that's occurring in reaction to what's going on in this world. I know that at the end of the day, "This too shall pass." Please be kind to yourself, your neighbors and respect yourself and others. Please consider the long term effects of your actions and consider slowing down, breathing and appreciating what you have. Please be considerate of those who are not as fortunate as you. Be compassionate and put yourself in others' shoes. Be a pillar of strength and support others, but reach out and ask for help if you need it too – as all we have is each other. Be impeccable with your words, be intentional in your actions and be thoughtful in your presence.

Twenty-twenty is the year that is going to make or break us. It was inevitable because of the way we have been operating as systems on overdrive and abusing life. Amid the COVID-19 pandemic, which has globally crippled thousand through sickness and fear with nation-wide quarantines, one of the most uplifting results was the usually dark and murky waterway canals in Venice turned noticeably brighter with dolphins, swans and signs of nature and life swimming through it! The water became clearer because there was less traffic and pollution on the canals. The air quality improved as well since there was less boat traffic than usual. In China, many overproducing factories of stopped during their pandemic quarantine and their usually polluted murky skies cleared to bright blue skies. Even during these challenging times, there is light at the end of the tunnel. Mother earth is healing, as humanity learns to improve.

IN CLOSING

Remember, there is no one ahead of you, nor anyone behind you. You are not more advanced than anyone else. You will always be a student learning every day. Until you eventually come to realize that you have become your teacher. Yet, everyone we meet, love, hurt, or serve and help are also our great teachers in life. From a child to elders, animals, to plants, everything has a reason and a meaning to teach and share.

To those who I haven't met yet, I don't know who you are, but I want to tell you that you are loved. I know you have been through a lot of difficult things, so thank you for being strong enough and pushing through. And even if you haven't felt your best lately, I'm so proud of you. But most importantly, you should be proud of yourself! You are loved, wanted and thus valid. You are enough.

You are irreplaceable.

I have been there too and I promise that everything will be okay someday. Maybe not tomorrow, but trust me - it will be okay. There are so many things in life to live for and so many things you haven't experienced yet. Remember that you are a survivor. You survived 100% of your best and worst days so far, so don't ever give up on yourself. Love the life that is in front of you, the life within you. Don't look back in regret. You lived through everything you did for a reason. Use your past as a guide, a compass and a roadmap. Don't be afraid to be yourself truly. People will choose to either love you or hate you. You will lose a few friends along the way. Those who stay love you for who you are. And they are the ones that matter.

If it weren't for all the teachers in my life, I would not be here today writing about my journey of overcoming and my story of triumph. I've experienced so many miracles in my life with the spirit of my grandparents, strength from my Mom & Dad, my soul sisters, blood sisters – Caroline & Anna, the sisterhood and brotherhood in 12 step programs and my son (my heart) Noah – who have all been the bedrock and foundation of my existence. I am deeply and profoundly grateful for you all. Although my paternal grandmother (Ba Noi) and maternal grandfather (Ong Ngoai) are no longer with us, I still hear their voices and feel their presence in my life. They are my ancestral guardians and guiding light.

To all the strong women who continuously remind me of the extraordinary strength, perseverance and unconditional love I have in life, I am beyond grateful for sisterhood with you. A special thank you to all the men who have come into my life and blessed me with their incredible strength in their life's journeys while teaching me so much about love and myself. I appreciate being in each of those relationships to grow into who I am today.

I am so proud of who I have become because of my father's hard work and dedication. As previously mentioned at the beginning of the book, Dad was awarded the "Best of the Best" in 2017 as the top bus operator out of 7,500 operators granted by the City of Los Angeles. He was nominated and given this award for consistently showing up on time, never missing a route, or even calling in sick for over 30 years of service. He taught us girls how to suit up and show up in life and be a useful member of society.

Being a refugee was not a choice. We were forced to flee a war-torn country. I was born during war-era and only a little girl when we escaped. I don't remember the war, but the crippling effects of war and trauma is a part of my genetic memory and DNA. It is an interwoven part of my family legacy and I am forever grateful that it is a part of my life's story.

The biggest adventure you can go on is living a life beyond your wildest dreams however that may look to you. I urge you to step outside your comfort zone and take significant action in the directions of your dreams. When you commit to a positive path and work tenaciously for a vision, the Universe will eventually conspire and orchestrate to help you. Even if it doesn't happen in the timing you hope and in the way you expect, it will happen in divine timing. Trust your path and know that love will guide you there.

I hope you will one day find your path, as I have found mine. I knew I needed to heal within first to help others. I needed to share my story. My hope was to at least help one person and to let people know they're not alone in this. I live a meaningful life today. I found faith in recovery at a time when nothing seemed to work.

I believe I was chosen by a higher destiny, to perform service to humankind, as we each have a calling and Soul purpose. When we genuinely listen to our souls calling and live in our life's purpose that is when life is most aligned, fulfilled and beautiful. It is when things fall into place because it is our destiny. This divine certainty happened in my home on "Memory lane," a sacred place of healing and unconditional love.

For months I invited and welcomed women and friends into my home to find refuge in the safe space I created for myself. We helped each other create a fellowship of sisterhood and friends who understand each other, where fear and loneliness vanished. We were held together by the never-ending strings of connection, love, concern and compassion for one another. God moves in mysterious ways for all of us.

Now is eternity, this very H.O.L.Y. Moment is eternity. For those of Us who have learned to live one day at a time, each Moment of life is a gift from God.

The Serenity Prayer is an important prayer I say throughout the day.

> *"God Grant Me the Serenity, to accept the Things I Cannot Change, the Courage to Change the Things I can and the Wisdom to know the Difference."* **—Neibuhr**

It has been said, Neibuhr first wrote the Serenity prayer as part of a sermon, where it spread to Alcoholics Anonymous. By 1936, the Serenity Prayer was well-circulated in 12-step recovery groups and has been referenced as a common prayer in literature. To this day, the prayer is utilized as a catch-all saying but is heavily used by groups to incentivize personal responsibility and calm in the face of adversity.

This prayer has saved me time and time again over the past 20 years. I was inflicted with so much shame, guilt and self-condemnation and relieved when I prayed this prayer. Inflicted with an obsession of the mind, I wasn't able to accept my life and my mind was out of control. Then, I finally allowed God to heal parts of my life; I wasn't able to do it on my own. Wherever you are in life and whatever you do, never forget to love yourself and to TRUST.

I've learned to be more mindful of the energy I let into my life. Now I choose places, partners and conversations wisely because I know they end up becoming who I am. We are who we allow into our sacred spaces. Our energies mix.

Beating cancer was incredible. Discovering I could beat something so overwhelming, realizing I wasn't alone and never giving up on my fight and journey was miraculous. I have overcome. I am still overcoming and am still walking forward on my journey of Life and Purpose. God will continue to disclose more to me and all of us. Every day I will continue to pray for the person who is still sick and suffering, or those who want to improve their quality of life. I will continue to trust my path and see that all my relationships are right and great things will come, as all future struggles will also pass. I will continue to work on myself daily and share what I've learned on my journey.

As I stand here at the open doorway now with clearer vision, the pure energy of love flowing and trueness of essence flowing through me, I know we will rise above together with knowledge, wisdom and truth. I stand alongside you to encourage you, inspire you, strengthen you and challenge you as we all travel along our unique journeys of becoming. May God bless you and keep you — until then. Until then, my friends, enjoy this wild ride that is *The Journey*!

Let this be an Awakening for all of Us.

We're in this together.

"7-DAY GUIDE TO SLOW LIVING""

How to Slow Down & Enjoy Life

We live in a fast-paced, hectic, overwhelming and continuously connected world, which affects the way that people experience life. Statistically speaking, we are unbalanced, overworked and experience chronic high levels of stress and sleepless. Even though connected virtually and electronically, we are feeling lonelier and more isolated than ever before. Our in-person relationships with others and our relationships with ourselves have a direct impact on our overall health and mental well-being and online links are not able to replicate the connectedness we need for a beautiful existence.

It's essential to take time to *slow down* and get centered and connect with our inner selves. At one point in our lives, we have all worked hard, struggled, suffered loss, been let down, forgotten, pushed aside and ignored. We can rise above this together with knowledge, wisdom and truth – and most importantly, you can live an extraordinary life that you love by *slowing down.*

More and more people are beginning to draw closer to a slower, more straightforward and *less hectic life* – especially during this time of change. We can see the popularity of concepts and methods, such as the Marie Kondo method of tidying up, tiny-house living, farmers' markets, minimalism, yoga, meditation, journaling and spiritual practices have become a popular way to connect with our inner selves. What all of this says is that we crave connectivity, inner peace and a slower pace of living. It's also a way to describe a feeling of cozy wellness. The following steps will take you through how you can start to look at your current lifestyle and identify what areas you may be able to make changes in immediately and what areas you may have to work towards in the future.

The following is a ***"7-Day Guide to Slow Living"*** to help you on your journey towards a new way of living, a slow living approach and enjoy every single day. These steps will help you connect the dots by looking at your current lifestyle and identify areas you may be able to change immediately and what you may have to work towards in the coming weeks ahead.

"7-DAY GUIDE TO SLOW LIVING""

DAY 1: MIND (SLOW-CARE)

"Smile, breathe and go slowly."
—Thich Nhat Hanh

DAY 1: The first step is to embrace a slower and more enjoyable way of living. Everything starts from the mind and then everything will flow into the self, spirit and soul. Take time to notice the recurring words that continuously repeat in your subconscious mind. The stories that you tell yourself that make you feel like you never have enough time each day that overwhelm you.

For example: *"I don't have enough time to get anything done today." "I feel so overwhelmed." "How am I going to get this done?"* These thoughts stem from limiting belief systems and the racket you have going on in your mind from the past. Write down your thoughts. This allows you to work through it. Notice and pay attention to any negative self-talk or inner dialogue that is not conducive to living a productive, positive, impactful life and that stops you from slowing down into your presence daily. Regardless of what your lifestyle/work/family may look like, you get to choose what you say to yourself daily.

What is the overall tone of your inner dialogue?

A positive mindset allows you to live in grace, poise, focus and inner calmness that is needed in everyday-life scenarios.

Slow-Care Guide: Practice by taking the time to *write down one to three good things that happened today at the end of each day that you are grateful for.* Journaling is a beautiful way to slow down the mind, as it allows you to take time to reflect while writing and purging. *Say kind words to yourself each morning and night.*

DAY 2: BODY (SELF-CARE)

"If anything is sacred, the human body is sacred."
—Walt Whitman

DAY 2: *How are you treating your body? Are you taking the time to create space around your meal times to appreciate your food? Are you treating your body with the respect it deserves by giving it self-care and consistent movement throughout the day?* Take time to care for yourself each morning. Create a morning routine that supports you. There is enough time in the day if you make time. Make time to eat meals, exercise and be gentle with yourself with self-care practices. We usually rush through the day without focusing on these crucial areas to keep our bodies healthy. Regardless of how hectic your life is, *there is no excuse* – you can squeeze in 5 -15 minutes to take care of yourself. Slowing down allows peak performers to be at the top of their game, gives them an edge and keeps them in the zone. Slowing down allows you to make healthier decisions and better choices because you can feel what is right for you. *Where do you think you could improve your body better? When was the last time you took care of yourself with self-care practices? Pampered yourself with a bath, face mask, long-walk technology-free at the beach?*

Self-Care Guide: Practice by taking time to *eat healthier, focus on your breath and detox from chemical dependencies.*

- ***Take 30 minutes of uninterrupted time for meals.*** Make more thoughtful food choices and create time to eat rather than rush through the day eating to feel satiated.
- ***Focus on your breath.*** Breathing can help prepare and recover the body during difficult Moments and when making critical decisions. Practice slowing down your breath. Take deep breaths and feel the air coming into your body and feel the stress going out. Focus on each breath and slow yourself down.
- ***Detoxing from chemicals and alcohol*** may be a great way to start the body's healing process. Avoid alcohol or any substances that will block energy frequencies.

DAY 3: SPIRIT (SOUL-CARE)

"The personal life deeply lived always expands into truths beyond itself." —**Anais Nin**

DAY 3: Focus on spiritual practices that soothe your soul. We often go throughout the day and forget to slow down to focus on spirituality. At this point, you feel good about where you are at in your life. You have a good sense of gratitude, but you feel like it can be better. You can always be better, do better and be more uplifted. Well, you're right. You have this feeling because you see how the potential of this reality can launch you into spiritual leaps and bounds. The reason why you don't have everything you want at this very Moment is that you were sending mixed signals to your mind, body and spirit. Now is the time to reshape your sense of perception and awareness to get clear on what you want and what holds you back within your soul.

Soul-Care Guide: Practice taking time to incorporate *prayer and meditation, affirmations, taking action and enjoyment into your daily life.*

- ***Prayer & Meditation:*** *Slowing down* allows you to create time for prayer and meditation. Prayer and meditation can come in many forms. It is connecting within to greater wisdom and Source, in whichever way resonates with you.
- ***Affirmations: Slowing down*** allows you to be mindful of your thoughts and create your life with statements that will support your growth. Taking time to say positive affirmations will let you feel better, help align your truth and vibrations in your body.
- ***Taking Action: Slowing down*** helps channel emotions to take actions that serve your higher self and lead to success in the long run. Take time to create Momentum on this day.

Day 4: LIFESTYLE (SACRED-CARE)

"The best and most beautiful things in the world cannot be seen or even touched. They must be felt with the heart"
—Helen Keller

DAY 4: The truth is that at this point in your life, you're fully capable of thriving, enjoying prosperity, creating the ideal state of living and thriving. You've already entered your country of purpose and self-realization is an integral part of your sacred awakening process on your journey. You should thank yourself for finally choosing you, the one and only, the pure love of your life. During this time, it is right for you to tap into the vastness of your innate gifts to experience breakthroughs you've been yearning for all your life.

Sacred-Care Guide: Make time to *harness, manage and distinguish your emotions to allow yourself to make better decisions and setting intentions.*

- ***Harness Emotions:*** Take time today to harness your emotions. Slowing down helps you harness the power of your feelings, helps guide you and take inventory of how you're feeling. Pay attention to what is going on within and around you.
- ***Manage Emotions***: *Slowing down* allows you to manage your emotions so they don't trigger poor choices, take unnecessary action or step back into old toxic behaviors.
- ***Distinguish Emotions:*** *Slowing down* allows you to feel, identify and distinguish the emotions you experience and will enable you to express those feelings.
- ***Better Decision Making:*** *Slowing down* allows your mind to assess circumstances to make better sound decisions.
- ***Setting Intentions***: *Slowing down* allows you to reflect and set your intentions throughout the day and become mindful of what it is that you're doing. Also, you will go forward with a clear and deep sense of clarity and purpose.

Day 5: ENVIRONMENT (SPACE-CARE)

"The more things you own, the more they own you."
—Anonymous

DAY 5: Whether you started your spiritual journey yesterday or ten years ago, we all continually need support in our living environment at work, home and school. There is a raw and real need to declutter and get the space around us to become as peaceful and refreshed as possible. The best way we can connect to the world around us is within us, but the influences of our environment are a vital part of our existence as well. Decluttering and eliminating unnecessary items around your living quarters and in your workspace is essential and the key to mental and spiritual health as well.

What do you no longer need in your life? Are there people, places and things that you may need to consider decluttering and removing from your life as well?

Space-Care Guide: Practice taking time to allocate the proper time to *declutter your life (people, places and things)* and *focus your energy on what matters most.*

- **Decluttering:** Take time to make conscious decisions to declutter your life, which includes toxic people, places and things – as well as emotional, mental and spiritual clutter.
- ***Time Allocation:*** Take time to allocate the proper time to organize your life. *Slowing down* allows you to carefully calculate and allocate your next move to observe challenges and opportunities that are in front of you as well.
- ***Focused Energy:*** Take time to focus on your energy in the proper areas that are most important. *Slowing down* allows you to see which direction you need to go to help you focus your energy on.

DAY 6: ENVIRONMENT (SCENIC-CARE)

"Love the world as your own self; then you can truly care for all things." —**Lao Tzu**

DAY 6: Paying attention to your environment is just as crucial as having clarity on the inside. Your body is a miracle vessel and your situation is the heaven that allows you to experience life on earth. Going into nature is essential to see and feel the vastness of this planet to help protect your beautiful soul and enable you to do all the beautiful things in this world.

Scenic-Care Guide: Take time to be in nature. Various activities will allow you to view the vast scenery our planet has to offer such, *as hiking, walking, camping, snowboarding, surfing, bike riding, golfing, mountain climbing, the list goes on and on.*

- ***Appreciate Nature:*** Slowing down allows you to enjoy the sensation of nature with water, wind and earth against your skin. Take deep breaths of fresh air outside while enjoying the serenity of trees, plants, birds and flowing water. You can also take nature walks, go for a swim, hike, Etc. You can try doing this daily with a loved one or by yourself. While many of us are shut in our offices, cars and homes most of the time, we rarely go outside to enjoy nature.

DAY 7: PEACE (SOLITUDE-CARE)

"You'll never find peace of mind until you listen to your heart." —**George Michael**

DAY 7: You made it! You've arrived at that place where everything feels right. Your heart is calm and your soul is lit. Your thoughts are positive and your vision is clear. You are finally at peace with your life. You are at peace with where you are and the direction you are headed. This ***"7-Day Guide to Slow Living"*** is designed to help heal aspects of your past, create better and healthier relationships, attract new opportunities, amplify your overall results and awaken the parts of you that you didn't even know existed. This guide will help you to attain peace of mind and help you manifest the life of your dreams. The perspectives and practices are suggestive only and brought to you from years of experience and personal research.

Solitude-Care Guide: Practice by enjoying some *rest, relaxation and creativity.* By practicing this, you will become *happy, joyous and free.*

- ***Rest and relaxation:*** Slowing down allows you to have time for rest and lowers stress, pressure, pain, fatigue and anxiety. Getting massages, taking bubble baths, power naps and gardening are great ways to get in some R&R (rest and relaxation).
- ***Creativity:*** Take time to focus on your creativity. Slowing down allows you to have the time to get creative, which includes painting, knitting, writing, etc.
- ***Happy, Joyous & Free:*** Slowing down allows you to be more comfortable, enjoy yourself and your life's journey on a whole level of freedom from living in the fast lane.

BONUS DAY 8

DAY-8 FRIENDS & FAMILY (SOCIAL-CARE)

"As we let our own light shine, we unconsciously give other people permission to do the same. As we are liberated from our fear, our presence automatically liberates others," —**Marianne Williamson**

DAY 8: Connectivity is one of the most important of human needs. We have been inherently social creatures with an online presence and in-person social communities. We are living in a fast-paced world and don't take the time to acknowledge each other's presence. It's essential to connect to survive and thrive in this beautiful life of ours.

CARE GUIDE: Practice taking the time to *spend quality time* with your loved ones; this includes *family, new and old friends, colleagues and loved ones.*

- ***Enjoyment:*** *Slowing down* allows you to create time to enjoy spending with loved ones and friends and to have fun. Friendship, connectivity and bonding are the keys to a happy life.
- ***Connectivity*:** *Slowing down* will allow you to make time to connect with those you love: your friends, family, colleagues and loved ones. Especially during times of struggle and imbalance, your friends and family will help balance you out.

We all have taken different paths to get where we are today. Everyone's way is different. No one can walk yours for you. If you follow these slow living steps, you will be able to see more clearly, be happier, stumble a little less and enjoy the views a lot more as you practice a life living a more *thoughtful life.* More importantly – you create the life you deserve through a genuine commitment to your purpose and your joy. Most importantly, you allow your life story to serve as one of your many spiritual guides in life.

AN OPEN LETTER TO MY SON, NOAH (AGE 11) (2/23/20)

"When you teach your son, you teach your son's son." —**The Talmud**

Dear Noah,

Thank you for everything you've done for me. *I love you so much, Sweetheart!* You have been the source of inspiration to help me get this book to the finish line and without your love, this book would not exist. Thank you for uplifting me, challenging me and helping me rise. You inspire me to be better and do better each waking H.O.L.Y. Moment. From the first moment I laid my eyes on you, my first journal entry about you and the last word I typed in this manuscript – you are the "One", my little "*Neo*". You are the most beautiful person inside out and I couldn't have asked for a more loving, caring and adorable son. As we continue to move forward on our journey together here are some simple reminders and a few words of advice and encouragement to help you navigate through our magical Kingdom.

First of all, always keep an open mind and heart. Remember to respect both men and women at all times. Women will lift you. Men will teach you how to be strong. Women will have your back and men will support you when you need it. Be the comfort to a broken girl's heart. Support another man's failure as they will be there for you when they succeed. Travel and see the world. Get out of your comfort zone. Learn from other cultures, people and truly explore this magical world we live in. Be the voice. Change the.cycle. Be the light.

Appreciate every experience that keeps you humble. Give back when you can. Create balance in your life. Keep your feet on the ground. Material things don't matter, but memories and people do. Try all the jobs. Try all the sports. Have a crack at everything. Learn it all; you'll never know what will spark your interest. Be active always. You're never too old to do anything. It's good for your body, good for your mind.

Trust your gut. You've always had that sixth sense since I can remember. It will be your guiding light. If violence is going down, just run, you won't get caught. Always run, you can sort it out later. If your teammates are there, assess the situation. Trust your instincts; they're spot on! Stand up for what you believe in, don't be muzzled. Protect your name. Stay away from drama and gossip. Don't ever slur someone online. Typing hurtful comments online is not ok. It's just the adult form of bullying. Be mindful. Get your facts right. There are three sides to every story.

Help carve out the future for the next generations to come. Lead by example amongst your family and friends. Have fun. Live your life. Learn a new language. Do whatever you like, but do it with love and kindness. Keep lighting up the room with your love and compassion. You are a strong and independent man.

Son, remember in order to have a life of great meaning, you have to leave a legacy. You have to leave behind an imprint of contribution. You have to have made a difference in some impactful way to others. The impact may be to a few or it may be to many, but it must be impactful either way. When it comes to the game of life, most of us like to play it as if it has no end. The decision of what you want to leave behind after your time on this planet is up, is one of the most important decisions you will ever make. Most people avoid this process because it is too uncomfortable. Yet for the ones that have the courage to embrace it, they are also the ones who live magnificent lives. So create your legacy and determine and reaffirm the imprint you intend for your life to leave.

Thank you for picking me to be your Mom. I'm here with you and always will be. Thank you for being my light and a part of my journey. I can't wait to see where you end up. You will be the light forever, my Son.

Love,
Mommy

AN OPEN LETTER TO HUMANITY (4/24/20)

"Love and compassion are necessities. Without them humanity cannot survive."—**Dalai Lama**

Dear Humanity,

It is time. I greet your soul with only love and compassion. Thank you for transforming the millions of lives on earth. I exist because you exist.

We've all come a long way.

As we enter into another day of being alive during the COVID-19 pandemic, I had another quiet morning break from work to be with family and with my own spirit. During my morning meditation I channeled my higher consciousness into form to write this letter to you.

I've been saddened with the news lately.

A pregnant woman dies with her fourth child when she contracted COVID-19. Her baby was delivered, but she loses her battle with infection before ever getting the chance to hold her newborn baby. In the wake of her death, grieving family members and friends hold a moment of silence and candle vigil.

Inside a youth prison, a 17 year-old calls his mom in desperation wondering how much longer he can avoid COVID-19 and nervously awaits his second test after residents fell ill around him. Prison officials stopped visitation, suspended schooling, ended counseling and locked some teens in solitary confinement for 23 hours a day to stem the outbreak. The unfolding medical crisis sickened inmates and staff members one-by-one. Thousands of adult inmates have been restricted from being released to head off the spread of the virus behind bars. Even in correctional facilities, the virus spread like wildfire.

"Be at peace. Don't worry about us anymore. Have fun in heaven! Love you so much!" a sister writes in tribute to her elder sister, a pediatric nurse who died on March 26 after battling the deadly virus.

Story's like this hit home and is a tragic loss for all of us right now. We are all a part of an unthinkably long list of families, friends, and strangers around the world that is changed forever by COVID-19.

Even though we are in isolation, our voice still matters.

No choice will ever be made in isolation.

I write to you today in what will go down in history as another terrifying pandemic that shut down the globe. We must stand today, as a great beacon of light for men, women, children – and millions of those who have been effected by COVID-19. Our life has been sadly crippled by the chains of this deadly virus.

We must stand as one as we are not guaranteed a tomorrow and we must continue the pursuit of happiness. It is obvious today this disease segregates no one. Not one citizen of any country, shade of your skin color, background, gender or religion. Instead we honor our sacred obligation to fight for all of humanity. We've come this far and we must demand freedom, love and respect for all.

Now is the time to make a real difference in the world in which we live. *Now* is the time to rise from hopelessness and walk on the path of faith. *Now* is the time to make peace with our families, friends, neighbors and for all of God's children. Now is the time to be the solid bed rock of humanity.

Twenty-twenty is not an end, but a beginning. Those who hoped for a better world will now be content knowing there will be a spiritual awakening as the world tries to slowly return to normal. We must not allow our creative protests, no matter how hate fueled it has been, to turn into physical violence. We must rise to the height of meeting physical force with soul force for the future of our children. We must protect them during this time, wrap them in our arms with love and comfort as we move through this trying time.

Our humanity must come together. We cannot walk alone. We must make the pledge that we shall always march ahead in the fight of the COVID-19 war. We cannot turn back. We must fight for the men, women, children who are stripped of their self-hood and fear of the future years after the dust from the pandemic settles down. We must make a stand for humanity.

Some of you are going through some great trials and tribulations. Some of you have experienced incredible loss. Loss of income, loss of self, loss of life, loss of hope, loss of faith, loss of respect for the government and society as a whole. Some of you have come from areas where your quest for spiritual and emotional freedom left you battered and staggered by the winds of brokenness. Continue to work with the faith that you have been redeemed on your painful journey as you read this. COVID-19 has changed all of us, but the situation will change. Change is inevitable. Let us not wallow in the valley of despair and hopelessness.

My friends, even though we face the difficulties of today and tomorrow, I still have faith. It is the faith that is deeply rooted from my journey that there is a pathway home. I have faith that our world will rise up and live out the meaning of our life's purpose and truth. I have faith that our globe will be transformed into an oasis of peace. I have faith that our children will live in a world where no fear and uncertainty will be the content of their character.

We will join hands with one another, look at one another in the eyes through our masks and have no fear of catching a disease that can be controlled with precautionary measures. We will pass the torch and this faith onto future generations. We will transform our nation into a beautiful symphony of sisterhood. We will be able to work together, to pray together, to struggle together, and stand up happy, joyous and free together. We will be free from the chains that binds our current world.

Let *humanity sing* from the hilltops, mountains, skyscraper, restaurant, business, home, and heart of everyone on this planet.

Let *humanity sing* with the hopes of our children responsibly rising from this pandemic, overcoming the hurdles of emotional rollercoasters, conquering the challenges of being socially distanced and crushing homeschool.

Let *humanity sing* from each door to door to help the hurt, support the weak and teach the young.

Let *humanity sing* from the voice of every parent, teacher, mentor, coach, and leader to share our wisdom passed on from ancestors to help our children grow up with continued compassion for the helpless and wounded.

Our humanity not only consists of every person who's alive right now, but also of everyone who's ever lived: an estimated 107 billion people. There are others who haven't been born yet – hopefully you will bring forth trillions more people.

From the core of my humble, imperfect humanity, I wish you happiness, love and a long, exciting journey.

Humanity is all of us.

All the best,
Cathy

NOTES & INDEX

PART ONE: Who You Thought You Were

CHAPTER FIVE: Mentors/Coaches/Sponsors/Gurus

- "The misuse of fear, excitement, sexual feelings, and sexual physiology to entangle another person."[3] A simpler and more encompassing definition is that traumatic bonding is: "a strong emotional attachment between an abused person and his or her abuser, formed as a result of the cycle of violence."[4]

- Patrick Carnes, Ph.D.. *The Betrayal Bond: Breaking Free of Exploitive Relationships*. Health Communications, Incorporated; 1 January 2010. ISBN 978-0-7573-9719-6

CHAPTER SIX: Thank God!

- *Lord's Prayer: "Lord, make me an instrument of your peace; where there is hatred, let me sow love; where there is injury, pardon; where there is discord, union; where there is doubt, faith; where there is despair, hope; where there is darkness, light; and where there is sadness, joy."* **~A prayer of St. Francis of Assisi**

REFLECTIONS ON THE 12 STEPS

- **12-Steps of Alcoholics Anonymous – Page 59-60, Big Book**

1. *We admitted we were powerless over alcohol—that our lives had become unmanageable.*
2. *Came to believe that a Power greater than ourselves could restore us to sanity.*
3. *Made a decision to turn our will and our lives over to the care of God as we understood Him.*
4. *Made a searching and fearless moral inventory of ourselves.*

5. *Admitted to God, to ourselves, and to another human being the exact nature of our wrongs.*
6. *Were entirely ready to have God remove all these defects of character.*
7. *Humbly asked Him to remove our shortcomings.*
8. *Made a list of all persons we had harmed, and became willing to make amends to them all.*
9. *Made direct amends to such people wherever possible, except when to do so would injure them or others.*
10. *Continued to take personal inventory and when we were wrong promptly admitted it.*
11. *Sought through prayer and meditation to improve our conscious contact with God as we understood Him, praying only for knowledge of His will for us and the power to carry that out.*
12. *Having had a spiritual awakening as the result of these steps, we tried to carry this message to alcoholics, and to practice these principles in all our affairs.*

WHAT IS HAVENING?

- "Havening Techniques (Havening), is a method, which is designed to change the brain to de-traumatize the memory and remove its negative effects from both our psyche and body," (Reference: www.havening.org).

- "Havening", is an innovative healing approach developed and created by Ronald Ruden, MD, PhD in collaboration with his brother Steven Ruden, DDS. (Reference: www.havening.org).

- "Havening can be described as a type of psycho-sensory modality based on the fields of neuroscience and neurobiology, which uses sensory input in order to alter thought, mood and behavior. It is believed that when an event or experience is perceived as traumatic or stressful, it becomes immutably encoded in the psyche and the body, often with life altering consequences," (Reference: www.havening.org).

- "This healing modality uses the foundation of neuroscience and neurobiology, which uses sensory input to alter thought, mood and behavior," (Reference: www.havening.org).

- "Havening, the transitive verb of the word haven, means to put into a safe place." (Reference: www.havening.org)

What is Your Baseline?

- Bottom & Top Line S.L.A.A. behaviors: **https://www.slaauk.org/useful-resources/slaa-how-documents/what-is-slaa-how/**

THE H.O.L.Y. MOMENTS©

- **H.O.L.Y. Moments© – Copyright by Cathy Trinh (2020)**

- GERD (Gastroesophageal Reflux Disease), which is a chronic digestive disease where the liquid content of the stomach refluxes into the esophagus and can be relived through diet and lifestyle changes. (Reference: www.webmd.com).

- **THE H.O.L.Y. MOMENTS©** Copyright 2020, Cathy Trinh

    - H. Holistic Moments
    - O. Organic Moments
    - L. Little Important Moments
    - Y. Yearned Moments

The Importance of *Slowing Down* in the COVID-19 "Coronavirus" Era:

- *Prayer: "God Grant Me the Serenity, to accept the Things I Cannot Change, the Courage to Change the Things I can and the Wisdom to know the Difference." -Neibuhr* ***"7-Day Guide to Slow Living"***"